D1300870

TOOLS OF THE
ANCIENT
ROMANS

A Kid's Guide to the History & Science of Life in Ancient Rome

RACHEL DICKINSON

nomad press

Cover image: Boris Kolomytsev, Toy Soldiers of Kolobob.

All illustrations by Shawn Braley

Photos: Scipio, courtesy of www.tu-berlin.de; Hannibal, courtesy of www.barca.fsnet.co.uk; Cato and Tiberius, courtesy of wikipedia.org; map of ancient Rome, courtesy of www.theaterofpompey. com; Shakespeare, courtesy of www.shakespeare.org.nz; other images courtesy of Planet Art

Nomad Press
A division of Nomad Communications
10 9 8 7 6 5 4 3 2
Copyright © 2006 by Nomad Press
All rights reserved.

ISBN: 0-9749344-5-3

Questions regarding the ordering of this book should be addressed to

Independent Publishers Group
814 N. Franklin St.
Chicago, IL 60610
www.ipgbook.com

Nomad Press
2456 Christian St.
White River Junction, VT 05001
www.nomadpress.net

Contents

Timeline

753 BCE: The city of Rome is founded by Romulus on the banks of the Tiber River.

507 BCE: The Roman Republic begins after the Romans overthrow the Etruscan kings.

450 BCE: The first Roman code of law, called the Twelve Tables, is published.

387 BCE: The Gauls, from what is now France, attack and plunder Rome. This may have driven the Romans to expand north to protect themselves from future invasions.

201 BCE: Rome defeats Carthage in the Second Punic War, giving Rome control over the western Mediterranean.

44 BCE: Julius Caesar declares himself "dictator for life." A large group of his fellow Senators aren't happy with that and have him assassinated, plunging Rome into chaos.

31 BCE: Octavian, Caesar's adopted son, defeats Mark Antony and Cleopatra at Actium, clearing the way for him to take the throne. Octavian takes the name Augustus. The Roman Empire, when Rome is ruled by emperors, begins.

30 BCE–180 CE: This period of time is often called Pax Romana or Roman Peace, because the empire enjoys relative peace and prosperity.

98–117 CE: Emperor Trajan rules the empire, which reaches its greatest size and power.

180–284 CE: With the death of Emperor Marcus Aurelius, the Roman Empire begins a steady slide into economic and political crisis. This period is sometimes called the "century of crisis."

284 CE: Diocletian becomes emperor and restructures the empire.

307–337 CE: Emperor Constantine I moves the capital of the Roman Empire from Rome to the city of Constantinople and makes Christianity the state religion.

370 CE: The Goths and other "barbarians" push into the northern Roman provinces when the Huns from Central Asia sweep into Eastern Europe, beginning a long period of invasions.

410 CE: The Visgoths, led by Alaric, sack the city of Rome.

476 CE: Odoacer, a German-born general, deposes the last Roman emperor, Romulus Augustulus, and becomes the first barbarian king. This is viewed as the end of the Roman Empire. The eastern half of the Roman Empire survived for another thousand years as the Byzantine Empire.

Romans All Around Us

WHY STUDY THE ROMAN EMPIRE? BECAUSE ITS influence lies all around you. From architecture and language to law and government, the Romans have influenced virtually every aspect of modern life.

Whenever you admire a beautiful classical public building—one with columns holding up a big triangular-shaped "pediment"—you're admiring Roman-inspired architecture. Wonderful feats of engineering like the development of the arch and the dome come directly from Rome. If you have been to Europe you may have actually driven on roads or traveled over bridges built two thousand years ago by Romans—bridges and roads that have withstood two thousand years of wind, rain, snow, war, and traffic.

Latin, the original language of ancient Rome, is now used for the official names of plants and animals and diseases—and it's also used in several legal terms. The real name for "chicken pox," for example, is the Latin word *varicella*. As far as modern legal terms go, alibi ("ala-bye"), subpoena ("su-peena"), and affidavit ("aff-ee-day-vit") are just a few . . . Still having a hard time believing that the language of ancient Rome is being used today? Look at the back of a nickel: the phrase: *E pluribus Unum* is Latin for "Out of many, one."

The founders of the United States turned to ancient Rome, particularly the writings of Cicero, when developing the new nation. In many ways, our government is structured much like the Roman Republic.

In *Tools of the Ancient Romans: A Kid's Guide to the History and Science of Life in Ancient Rome* you'll learn the importance and relevance of ancient Rome to our everyday lives. You'll also learn what life was like for all types of Romans in a world of gladiators and gods and goddesses, extreme poverty and great wealth, and momentous discovery. This book will give you a taste and feel of this world through activities that transport you back in time. So get your imagination ready and see what it was like to be a Roman kid, adult, senator, or slave. When you come back to the present day and look around you, you'll see that ancient Rome has been with you all along.

Learn the story of the founding of Rome

Explore the history of the earliest Roman tribes

Uncover your own family history

Fantastic Beginnings

THE ROMAN EMPIRE SEEMS VERY DISTANT AND FOREIGN TO us today, but at its greatest strength, almost 2,000 years ago, it was the mightiest empire in the world. Nearly 60 million people lived under Roman rule in lands stretching from **Asia Minor** and Africa to Britain, about the same size as the United States. How did such a huge empire begin? It all starts with the humble and mysterious origin of Rome, the mighty city that sits on the banks of the Tiber River. The history of Rome is a fascinating mix of fact and fiction, combining archeological and scientific discoveries with ancient stories about gods and goddesses, mortals and murders, cruel kings and lost civilizations.

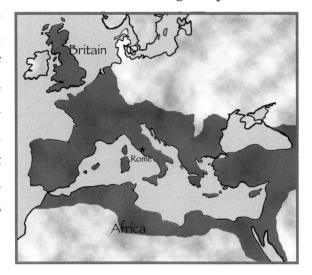

Location, Location, Location

Geographically speaking, Rome was perfectly sited to become a great city-state. If you look at a map of modern Italy, you'll find Rome on the west coast of the peninsula that juts smack dab into the Mediterranean Sea. Its location at the mouth of the Tiber River meant that the ancient city of Rome controlled the port there and was able to trade with both northern

and southern neighbors, as well as regions to the west. The Tiber River also provided a convenient place from which to launch a navy, enhancing the military might of the Romans. The mountain range to the north (today the Alps of northern Italy) effectively cut the Romans off from invaders north of the peninsula in the days before planes, trains, and automobiles. Today, Rome is spread over seven hills nestled beside the banks of the Tiber River, but in ancient times, when the city was smaller, people lived on the hilltops. Those hills provided a military advantage—allowing Romans to see and protect themselves from their enemies as they approached from below.

How It All Began: The Story of Romulus and Remus

Rome, the ancient Romans maintain, was founded by Romulus, who became its first king in 753 BCE. But in order to understand where Romulus fits in, you have to push the beginnings of Rome back even further—back to the destruction of the city-state of Troy in about 1200 BCE. (Archeologists

KNOW YOUR ANCIENT ROMAN *Geography*

Asia Minor: A peninsula of western Asia between the Black Sea, the Aegean Sea, and the Mediterranean Sea. In ancient times, it was where most Eastern and Western civilizations intersected.

have uncovered the remains of an ancient city in modern Turkey that they believe was Troy.) The Roman poet, **Virgil**, described the destruction of Troy in the most famous poem of the Roman era, *Aeneid*. In the poem, Aeneas, the son of the Roman goddess Venus and a mortal man, fights against the Greeks in the Trojan Wars. When the great city of Troy falls, Aeneas flees and escapes with his life. After a long journey, he lands in Latium, a city on the banks of the Tiber River. Through a series of fantastic events, Aeneas marries a beautiful princess and becomes an ally of the neighboring Etruscans.

The Trojan Horse

The Greek army left a hollow horse, filled with Greek soldiers, outside the gate of the city of Troy. Thinking the horse was a gift from the gods, the Trojans brought the horse into the city. That night the Greek soldiers came out and opened the city gates to the entire Greek army. After years of trying to break into the city the Greeks won the war by tricking the Trojans.

Virgil's poem goes on to tell the story of Aeneas's family over the course of hundreds of years, including the birth of the twins Romulus and Remus, in the eighth century BCE. Their mother is the beautiful Rhea Silvia, a descendent of Aeneas, and their father is the god Mars. Poor Rhea Silvia is thrown into the river by an angry uncle and the baby twins set adrift in the Tiber River in a reed basket. The basket becomes caught on a fig branch and the twins end up in the care of a she-wolf. Eventually, a shepherd finds the boys and raises them as his sons.

When the boys grow older, they decide to return to where they were rescued from

The she-wolf nursing Romulus and Remus.

How the Years Work

BCE refers to the time "before the common era," and it is used as a non-religious replacement for BC, which means "before the birth of Christ." The Romans were Christians and invented our calendar, which uses the birth of Christ as the major landmark of time. Around 545 CE, a Roman monk named Dionysius Exiguus, wanted to improve the reckoning of the date of Easter, and came up with the present system of identifying a date from the time of the birth of Jesus. The numbers for the years before the common era are like a countdown toward the birth of Jesus. For example, if someone was born in 120 BCE and died at age 45, the year of death would be 75 BCE. The year 120 BCE occurred before the year 75 BCE, and the fifth century BCE comes before the fourth century BCE.

After the birth of Christ the years are called CE for "common era." This is also a non-religious substitute for AD, which stands for anno Domini, "in the year of our Lord." In CE, as the years pass, the numbers get higher. For example, 1910 occurred 30 years before 1940. And the third century CE comes before the fourth century CE.

Today, it is becoming more common to use the more modern and non-religious names of BCE and CE for BC and AD.

the river, because they want to create a city on that spot. By reading the omens told in the flights of birds (more on omens later), they decide to build their city on Palatine Hill—one of the seven hills of Rome—and that Romulus will be king. Remus is not thrilled about this because he also wants to be king. As Romulus is marking out the city's boundaries, Remus teases him, making him angry. In a fit of temper, Romulus kills his brother and builds the city himself.

This new little city, called Rome after Romulus, has almost no women in it, so Romulus invites the neighboring tribe, the Sabines, to a harvest festival. He then kidnaps 600 young Sabine women and sends the Sabine men packing. According to the story, when the Sabine men come back to recapture their women, the women tell them they want to stay and persuade the Romans and the Sabines to work together.

While this is a good story, it is probably not true. We do know, however, that the people we know as the ancient Romans were a mix of many different ethnic and cultural groups.

How the Archeologists Tell the Story

Virgil's version of the founding of Rome is one of the most famous stories in ancient literature, and art and architecture throughout Rome pay tribute to the twins Romulus and Remus. Parts of Virgil's story may be based on fact, but it's pretty unlikely that Romulus and Remus were the sons of gods or that they were raised by wolves. What archeologists have discovered, though, is evidence that by the late 600s BCE, large private houses, public buildings, and even public-works projects were being built in the area of Rome. Romans were remarkably good at building things like baths, aqueducts, sewers, monuments, buildings, and roads, and when archeologists dig down to uncover the past they find many things left behind by the builders of this great empire.

A Person's Trash is an Archeologist's Treasure

Archeologists can learn an enormous amount about ancient cultures by digging through the trash they left behind. Think about what you could tell about an area if you dug a pit in your backyard and uncovered parts of old toys, pieces of dishes, perhaps some old bottles, some bricks, or maybe even a piece of a foundation. As an archeologist you would carefully document where you found each item and then try to "read" what the items told you. What did the pattern on the broken dish tell you about when it was made? Was the toy made from plastic or metal? What kind of cement was used in the foundation? These are the types of clues archeologists use to piece together the past.

names *you should know*

Virgil [Publius Vergilius Maro] (70–19 BCE) Famous Roman poet who wrote the history of the founding of Rome, called *Aeneid*.

One of the most remarkable structures archaeologists have uncovered is the Cloaca Maxima, which was a big pipe that drained the marshy areas around the Roman Forum. This pipe ran to the Tiber River and was built in the sixth century BCE. During this time period, the city of Rome was developing from a place of straw-roofed huts to a city of substantial buildings with tiled roofs, monuments, and a paved marketplace in the area of the Forum. How do we know all this? Archeologists have dug down below the modern-day Forum and uncovered the foundations of some of these earlier structures.

The Cloaca Maxima is used as a sewer today.

Q: What *language* did Romans speak?

Rome as a Melting Pot

So who were these early builders and shapers of what was to become the most powerful city in the world? In the sixth century BCE, the Italian penisula was populated by a number

The Etruscans

Today the Etruscans are a mysterious, ancient civilization. We know what some of their buildings, monuments, and elaborate burial tombs looked like through archeological excavations, and from this we can guess that they were, at some point, successful seafaring traders and merchants. We also know that they didn't speak Latin, the language of the Romans, but that's about it. Very few examples of Etruscan writing exist today—O?Q43T—mainly just inscriptions on gravestones. The area the Etruscans once occupied in the north of Italy is today called Tuscany, which comes from the Latin name for the Etruscans—Tursci.

Although there were times when the Etruscans and Romans found themselves allies against a common enemy, the overthrow of Tarquin the Proud signaled the beginning of the end of the Etruscan civilization. The Etruscans had been responsible for creating many public institutions and buildings in Rome, but they found themselves constantly at war with the great city they once controlled. By the first century CE, the Etruscan civilization completely disappeared as Rome exerted its control over the entire Italian peninsula.

Q: Who built the *Cloaca Maxima?*

of different tribes of people. Some tribes, like the Etruscans, the Carthaginians, and the Greeks, controlled great expanses of land: the Etruscans controlled the north, the Carthaginians ruled the lands to the west in Africa, and the Greeks controlled the lands to the south. The Latins, the tribe from which the Romans came, lived between the Etruscans and the Greeks. Other tribes included people known as Sabines (whose women starred in Virgil's story of the founding of Rome) and Sammites, who had very small tracts of land.

All of these tribes contributed to the rise of the city of Rome, much the way immigrants from around the world have contributed to the success of the United States. Early Rome was very much a melting pot of cultures. Many of the biggest early building projects in Rome, including the Cloaca Maxima, were built by the Etruscans, who also gave Rome many of its early kings. To the south, the Greeks were creating settlements, bringing Romans into contact with some fundamental skills like reading and writing, and more complicated and sophisticated ideas about architecture, art, and mythology.

Early Rome and the Reign of Kings

After Romulus, the first king, a series of seven kings ruled Rome. Some of these kings may be fictional characters and some may be real, but all of them are part of the traditional story of Rome's beginning. Several

Q: Who were *Romulus* and *Remus?*

kings after Romulus's reign were responsible for enlarging the city, building religious temples, and calming down the neighboring Sabines (who were apparently still upset over their women being stolen at that harvest festival). The fourth king, Tullus Hostilius (673–642 BCE) is believed to have built Rome's senate house, which later became very important. The sixth, seventh, and eighth kings were all Etruscans. They

activity: **Uncovering You**

Like the stories surrounding the beginnings of Rome, most families have stories that have been passed down from generation to generation that may or may not be completely true.

These could be stories about how great-uncle Matt was a horse thief in Montana, or how grandmother Elsie saved the family jewels by sewing them into the hem of her coat when she got on a boat to come to America. Think about how stories are often passed down by word of mouth and consider the fact that along the way they might have gained a few interesting details.

In this activity you'll uncover some of the fact and fiction of your own family history. The goal is to learn something about your family that you didn't know before, and then to write it down.

1 First, make a list of all your living relatives.

2 Now choose at least six people to interview. You can concentrate on one side of the family (your mother's people or your father's people) or do both. You are the combination of both sides of the family and get to inherit all the stories! Interview older relatives like grandparents and great-aunts and uncles if you can.

3 Make up a list of questions to ask when you interview. Here are some ideas:

- What is your full name and when and where were you born?
- If married, when and where did you get married and what is the name of your spouse?
- If you have children, what are the full names of your children and when and where were they born?
- Tell me one story from your childhood.
- Tell me one family story that your parents or grandparents told you when you were a child.
- Are there any family stories you've heard that you think are particularly interesting?

supplies

relatives
pad of paper
pen or pencil
tape recorder
tapes

amily History
— Fact and Fiction

4 Conduct your interviews. Make sure to tape record them if you can. If you're unsure of the spelling of a name, ask the person to spell it for you.

Have fun! Family stories are so interesting and you're bound to learn a lot of things you never knew before.

5 Compare the stories of different relatives. If you interviewed several relatives from the same side of the family, there are bound to be some stories that come up several times.

6 Once you've heard a story from one person ask others about it. It's interesting when you get different versions, sometimes really different versions. See if you can figure out which stories seem more like fiction than fact.

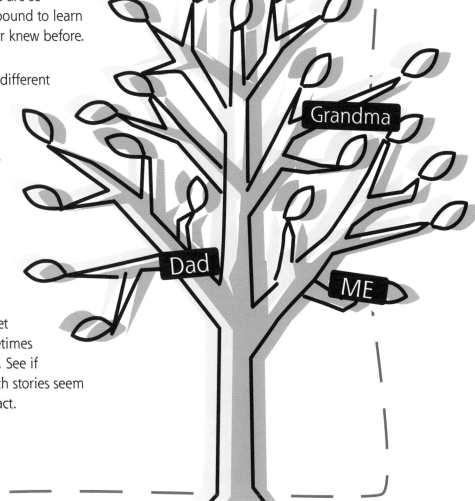

made a lot of improvements to the little city. In addition to the Cloaca Maxima, they built temples and a fortification wall around the city, called the **Servian wall** after King Servius Tullius (578–535 BCE).

The eighth and last Roman king was Lucius Tarquinius Superbus, or Tarquin the Proud (535–509 BCE). He became king through treachery and ruled cruelly. Tarquin's wife, the daughter of King Servius, convinced her husband to have her father assassinated so that Tarquin could be king. Tarquin was an arrogant man who had a rotten son named Sextus. Sextus raped his cousin's wife, Lucretia, who then killed herself. Another cousin, Brutus (not the famous Brutus we learn about later), heard about this horrible act and got together enough people to start a rebellion to drive the Tarquins from power. He succeeded and that was the end of the reign of kings in Rome.

Q: Who was the *last king* of Rome?

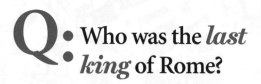

KNOW YOUR ROMAN *Architecture*

aqueduct: a pipe or channel that carries water from its source to a city.

Cloaca Maxima: a huge pipe, built in the sixth century to drain the Roman marshlands as well as public toilets, bathhouses, and other public buildings.

Roman forum: the main meeting place in a Roman city; surrounded by government buildings, courts, and temples.

Servian wall: a fortification wall built around Rome in the fourth century BCE, named after the Etruscan King Servius Tullius (578–535 BCE).

Learn the structure of the early Republican government

See how wealth determined a Roman's rights

Glimpse the plight of slaves and the life they endured

The Roman Republic —Democracy Rules . . . or does it?

AFTER THE LAST KING, TARQUIN THE PROUD, WAS DRIVEN from office, Rome became a **republic**, which means a government of elected representatives. It was governed by the **Senate**, the **Centuriate Assembly**, and two **consuls**, who in some

ways replaced the king. The consuls were elected every year by the assembly. They had the power to declare war and enforce laws. This power was called **imperium**. The Senate was a group of advisors that had existed before the republic, during the time of the kings. The king could choose to listen to the senators, but he was under no legal obligation to take their advice.

The word republic comes from the Latin word *res publica*, which means "commonwealth" or "state." But just because Rome was called a republic doesn't mean that it was a democratic government the way we think of one today. Most Romans did not go to vote and elect people to represent them in government. As you'll see, it was a complicated system, but it worked.

Three Separate Classes

To understand the system of government in Rome, it helps to first understand Roman class structure. Roman citizens were born into one of three classes.

Romans from wealthy families who had been in Rome for a long time were called **patricians** (after the word *patres*, which meant "fathers"). Accordingly, they were considered father figures, or leaders, of Rome. Patricians thought themselves superior to people who didn't have a lot of money. For many years, only the patricians could serve in the Senate.

Beneath the patricians on the social ladder were the **equites**. Equites did not have as much money as the patricians. Originally knights, they were the businessmen of the day—merchants and bankers—and today we would probably characterize them as Rome's middle class. The name

KNOW YOUR ANCIENT ROMAN *Government*

republic: a form of government with elected representatives.

Senate: a group of wealthy men who made laws when Rome was a republic, and advised the king or emperor when Rome was a monarchy and empire.

Centuriate Assembly: a branch of the Roman Senate that included both patricians and plebians, though only the wealthy members' votes counted.

consul: one of two head magistrates of Rome elected every year—consuls held imperium.

imperium: the power to declare war and enforce laws.

equite comes from the Latin word equis for horse. In order to be an equite, you needed to have enough money to buy a horse.

The lowest class of Roman citizen was the plebeian class. They were freeborn citizens who worked hard but didn't have a lot of money. Some of them even had to beg for food to survive. If plebeians lived in the city, and were lucky enough to have a job, they might do something like sell food at one of the many food stalls, or run a small shop. Plebeians who lived in the country might live on a small farm where they made little money but grew enough food to feed their family.

Women, no matter what class they fell into, were not allowed to participate in politics at all during the early days of the republic. A woman had to do whatever her paterfamilias (male head of household) said. If a woman was married, her paterfamilias was her husband, otherwise it was her father or the oldest man in her immediate family. Although Roman women were citizens under Roman law (unless they were slaves), Roman law was not very fair to them: women were not allowed to vote and men in government believed that women should be absolutely under male control. Even the most respectable of women were expected to remain in their homes, out of the public eye. Their duty was to keep or manage the home.

Q: **Name the three classes of** *Roman citizens.*

As time went on, though, things began to change. With thousands of husbands killed in war or away on military campaigns, many women were forced to take up their missing husband's roles. They inherited and took control of their husbands' money—a responsibility that required they leave the house and assert themselves in public. They met with other women—and men—to discuss their affairs, attended lectures, and began to host their own guests. While this movement gained momentum, women began to appear as the main subjects in works of art. More attention of every kind resulted in more rights and freedoms for women.

Then There Were the Slaves

The final group of people in Rome were the slaves. While some slaves were better off than some plebeians because they had a roof over their head and food to eat, they were not considered citizens (plebeians were) so they were not protected by Roman law if they were beaten or abused by their master. Slavery was a fact of life 2,000 years ago. Some wealthy Romans owned hundreds or even thousands of slaves. Historians have estimated that slaves may have made up as much as one-third of the total population on the Italian peninsula.

Q: Why did women begin to have *rights* and *freedom*

Slave Markets

Rome relied heavily on slavery. Aside from the labor slaves provided for large agricultural estates, as well as in mines and households, they also held many different jobs in the ever-growing city of Rome.

Huge numbers of war prisoners periodically added to the slave population, including 30,000 from a victory against Tarentum in 209 BCE, and 50,000 from Carthage as a result of the First Punic War in 146 BCE. But war prisoners didn't supply enough to satisfy the demand for slaves, so slave markets were set up. The slave trade developed into a big business as adults and children were kidnapped throughout the Mediterranean world and sold into slavery. At one market, over 10,000 slaves were sold every day.

Roman Citizens

Being a citizen in ancient Rome was a big deal because it meant you had rights under the laws. Originally, to be a Roman citizen, both your parents had to be Roman. Sometimes, the Senate granted citizenship to individuals or foreigners as a special legislative act (this was particularly true if the foreigners were bringing a lot of money or influence with them to Rome).

Roman citizens were expected to pay taxes and serve in the army. In return, they had the right to vote for representatives, could form contracts, had the protection of the courts, and could be eligible to hold office.

As the years went on, being a Roman citizen gave a man a great deal of protection both in Rome and throughout the empire. Citizens were entitled to return to Rome to stand trial. For example, a man named Paul, an early Christian who is credited with organizing the Catholic Church, was about to be executed in Jerusalem. He stated, *civis Romanus sum*—"I am a Roman citizen"—and was returned to Rome for trial.

Who were the slaves? Romans who didn't pay their debts, prisoners of war, descendents of slaves, or children who'd been abandoned by families too poor to feed them. Slaves were not considered people—they were considered property.

The Roman Government

Now that you understand how people were divided up in the Roman republic, you can learn how the government worked. The most dominant branch of government was the Senate, which was first made up of 100 patricians (later 300, then 600) from the richest and oldest families of Rome. Even if equites and plebeians had been permitted to become senators, they wouldn't have had enough money to do so, because senators were not allowed to have jobs on the side. The duty of the senator was to debate and recommend policy, and to decide which territories should be made provinces and come under Roman law. They kept their eye on the big picture.

The Centuriate Assembly, on the other hand, ran the day-to-day business of the republic. They chose all the magistrates that were in charge of the different parts of the republic. Initially, members of this assembly were elected by those with lots of money. As a result, the laws they passed, and the magistrates they chose, favored the rich people.

civis Romanus sum
"I am a Roman citizen"

Consuls were the chief magistrates appointed by the Centuriate Assembly. For most of the Roman Republic, only patricians could be consuls. With their power of imperium they could order executions and floggings, draft citizens into the military, and command armies on military campaigns. The Romans didn't have professional generals, so the consuls were in charge of the armies. The reason the Romans elected two consuls was to ensure that no one man held absolute power, but the problem was that there were times when the two consuls didn't agree. These occasions led to breakdowns in the power structure and chaos.

Over the years, the Centuriate Assembly added several magistrate positions to help run the republic, including censors, praetors, aediles, and quaestors. Censors took an annual census of citizens (counting all the citizens), praetors were the judges, aediles were the administrators, and the quaestors kept track of the money. They made sure everything was running smoothly in the city of Rome while the consuls were out commanding the armies and the Senate was debating the big picture.

KNOW YOUR ANCIENT ROMAN *People*

patricians:	wealthy Romans	**plebians:**	poor Romans
equites:	knights, later businessmen and merchants	**slaves:**	people who were owned by wealthy Romans

The Twelve Tables

Roman law was passed down through word of mouth over the years, but between the years 451 and 449 BCE, the laws of Rome were finally published as the Twelve Tables on bronze plaques that were posted in the Forum. These laws applied to everyone. For centuries afterward, every Roman boy memorized the laws in the Twelve Tables as part of his education. We don't even know how many laws were written on the Twelve Tables because the original tablets were destroyed by the Gauls when they sacked Rome in the fourth century BCE. However, some snippets survived through oral tradition. Here are a couple of the more unusual laws:

If a thief broke into your house at night you could kill him. However, if he tried to rob your house during the day, you couldn't kill him unless he resisted you with weapons.

You are forbidden to put gold in a funeral pyre. However, if a person's teeth had been held in place by gold bridgework, it was not necessary to remove it before cremation.

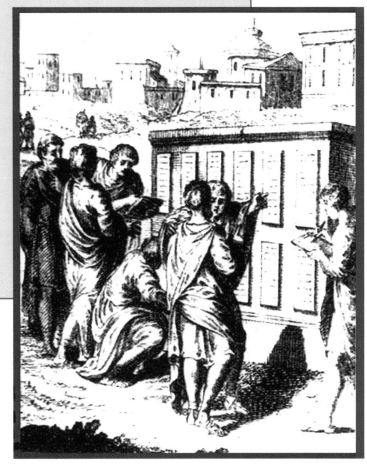

Anyone caught singing or circulating insulting songs about someone could be clubbed to death (this law must have been amended when the form of entertainment known as satire came into being).

If a father gives up his son for sale three times, the son shall be free.

Q: How did *a slave* become a slave?

activity: **Writing Tablet**

Educated Romans used wax writing tablets that could be used over and over. All they had to do was smooth their old message over to start again.

1 Measure and cut three pieces of foamboard that are 10 inches by 8 inches. USE YOUR XACTO KNIFE WITH CAUTION!

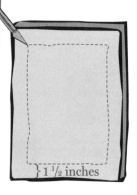

{ 1 ½ inches

2 Take one of the foamboard rectangles and measure 1½ inches all the way around the edge. Now cut out the middle. You should end up with something that looks like a picture frame.

3 Place the frame on one of the solid rectangles and glue it in place.

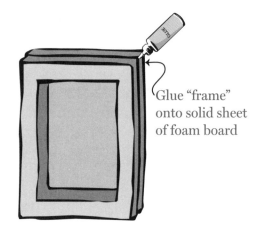

Glue "frame" onto solid sheet of foam board

supplies

foamboard
(at least ¼ inch thick)

ruler

Xacto knife

glue

pen

string or leather thong, two pieces about 6 inches long each

Play-doh *(the kind that stays soft)*

bamboo skewer

markers

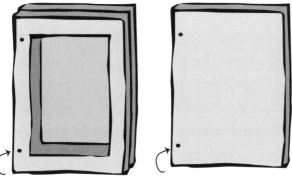

Measure ½ inch from left edge and 2 inches from top and bottom, and make holes

4 Measure in ½ inch from the left long edge and make a dot two inches from the top and the bottom on both the single piece of foam board and the one that's been glued. You're going to make holes here so you can attach the front cover to your writing tablet.

5 Make a hole by pushing the pen carefully through the foamboard and twisting.

6 Attach the cover to the tablet and tie with the string.

7 Take the Play-doh and carefully fill the area between the frame and the back cover. You should end up with a smooth surface.

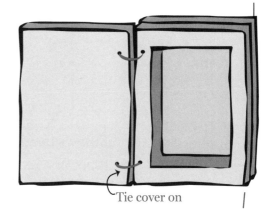

Tie cover on

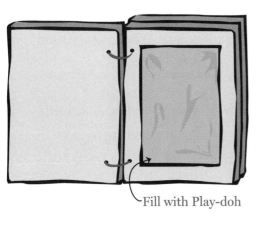

Fill with Play-doh

8 You can write on your tablet with the bamboo skewer and then smooth it over when you're finished.

9 Decorate the cover of your writing tablet with markers to make it your own!

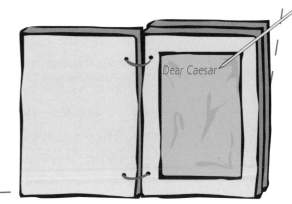

Dear Caesar

Interesting Tidbit:
Fasces

Fasces are bundles of wooden rods tied around a double axe with a red ribbon. Punishment is represented by the rods and execution by the axe. These were the symbols of imperium held by the consuls.

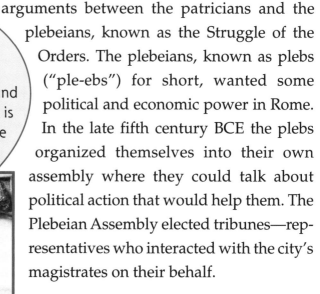

The early years of the republic were dominated by arguments between the patricians and the plebeians, known as the Struggle of the Orders. The plebeians, known as plebs ("ple-ebs") for short, wanted some political and economic power in Rome. In the late fifth century BCE the plebs organized themselves into their own assembly where they could talk about political action that would help them. The Plebeian Assembly elected tribunes—representatives who interacted with the city's magistrates on their behalf.

It took 200 years, but eventually, the Plebeian Assembly gained the respect of Rome's magistrates, the Centuriate Assembly, and even the Senate, and it became recognized as a legitimate branch of the Roman government. When this happened, the tribunes the Plebeian Assembly elected were given the right of veto, meaning they could say, "I forbid this," to laws or acts that went against the interests of the plebeians. The laws passed were imposed upon all Roman citizens—not just the plebs.

Q: What was the *Struggle of the Orders?*

The triumph of the Plebeian Assembly contributed to the expanding rights of plebeians throughout Rome. Initially, a tribune was the highest office a pleb could hold, but by the third century BCE, the wealthiest plebeians were gaining seats in the Centuriate Assembly. As the years of the republic wore on, the plebeians—and even the equites—demanded and gained more power from the patricians. They accomplished this peacefully, which freed the Romans to concentrate on conquering new territories and expanding its borders.

Follow Rome's
expanding roads
as the republic
grows

See why Rome
made friends
of conquered
enemies

Learn about
the elephants
that marched
on Rome

Expanding the Roman Republic

MUCH OF THE HISTORY OF ANCIENT ROME IS ABOUT military conquest. Right from the founding of the ancient city, the leaders seemed to have an unstoppable need to conquer and control more and more territory and people (remember what Romulus did when he wanted women for his city—he kidnapped them). The conquest began with the land surrounding the city of Rome.

Rome was the northernmost city in Latium, which is what the land in the central western part of the Italian peninsula was called. Latium contained about 30 communities, which banded together to create the Latin

The Roman Republic, 338 BCE.

Roads

You might have heard the saying, "All roads lead to Rome." Well, during the Roman republic and empire this was literally true. All the roads in Roman territory, which at one time was most of Europe, were somehow linked to the city of Rome.

League. This organization was a way for the communities to provide military protection for each other. But right from the start, Rome tried to dominate the league.

Rome Takes Over

During the fifth and fourth centuries BCE, the Romans conquered huge parts of the central section of the Italian peninsula, which made their Latin League neighbors pretty nervous. And, as they feared, by 338 BCE, Rome had become strong and threatening enough that they annexed most of the Latin League communities. This means that they took control over everyone around them. The league was abolished and its communities came under the rule of the Roman Republic. People living in these communities had to abandon their local Latin dialects and adopt the Roman dialect, which became the surviving form of Latin. The leaders of Rome were smart about this annexation. They made the wealthy citizens from the newly acquired towns part of Roman nobility, which allowed them to hold political offices. Because of this political involvement, the Latins from the annexed communities soon became Rome's strongest allies.

Q: What was the *Latin League?*

It wasn't long before Rome conquered the rest of Italy and set up treaties with all the new territories. The way these treaties worked was pretty clever. Rome allowed these annexed territories to keep control over a lot of what was happening in their own communities, even though they officially became territories of Rome. The Roman territories sent money to Rome—because everyone was taxed by Rome—and they also supplied men for the military. This is kind of like our system of state and federal government. Each American state makes laws that govern what happens in each state, yet the federal government gets to make laws that affect everyone in the country (and they also collect taxes from everyone!).

Q: How did Rome *win over* the towns they *conquered?*

"All roads lead to Rome"

Wherever Romans went, they tried to "Romanize" the locals. How did they do this? Roman citizens were sent to live in outposts, or Roman communities, in the new territories. Many of these outposts were near Roman military bases, which offered protection to the people living there. Roads were built to connect the city of Rome to the territories. The roads helped bring the empire together and helped maintain order (because the Roman army could travel quickly to any trouble spots). They also served as "highways" to help spread the Roman language and culture. Eventually, Roman roads connected every corner of the vast Roman empire.

Soon the Roman Republic reached beyond the Italian peninsula in their search for new territories to conquer. Raiding foreign towns and enslaving the population became a very profitable activity for wealthy Roman military officers. Remember, elected consuls headed military campaigns, and they made

The Via Appia

The first Roman road was the Via Appia, which connected Rome with Capua and southern Italy. Built in 312 BCE by Appius Claudius Caecus, this road was 132 miles long. This was the most famous road in the Roman Republic, and by the end of the second century BCE, it was paved. If you go to Italy you can drive on a 2,000-year-old road because parts of the Via Appia, which is also known as the Appian Way, are still visible and in use today!

activity: Toga

*Togas were the classic garb of every Roman man.
It was both dress-up and everyday wear.*

1 Buy four yards of fabric at a fabric store. (or cut a bedsheet in half.) If you want to be authentic, buy some off-white muslin fabric.

2 Put on shorts and a T-shirt. Place three-quarters of the fabric over your left shoulder so it hangs down to your ankles or so in the front.

3 Pull the longer end of the fabric loosely across your back and under your right arm, then drape it over your left shoulder.

4 Take the shorter end of the fabric (the piece that hangs to your ankles in front) and pin it to the fabric under your right arm. It sounds more complicated than it is—just try it. The key is to keep your right arm free.

5 Pin your brooch (see next activity) through the fabric on your left shoulder to hold it all in place.

supplies

piece of fabric
4 or 5 yards long

safety pins

brooch

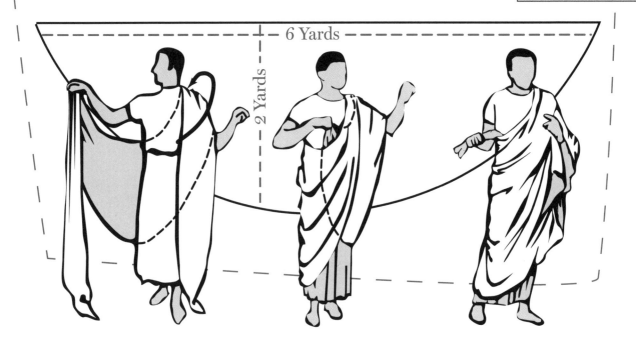

6 Yards

2 Yards

activity: **Brooch**

supplies

fimo or sculpy clay
(four or five colors)

plastic knife or wooden tools for clay

glue

pin backs
(available at a craft store)

Romans, both men and women, used brooches to pin their togas at the left shoulder. These are really fun to make—you're only limited by your imagination.

1 Soften pieces of the clay by kneading it with your fingers.

about 1/4 inch

2 Make a ball of clay in your hand, then mush it down on a flat surface to make either an oval or round shape. Flatten it so that it's about ¼ inch thick. This is the base for your pin.

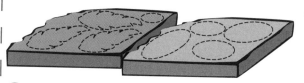

3 Soften up pieces of clay from all the different colors you have. Now make your design on your base. You could make leaves by flattening out a piece of green clay and cutting the shapes with a plastic knife. A simple flower can be made by rolling pieces of clay into little balls and then flattening them slightly on the base. You can do landscapes, portraits, designs. Go nuts!

4 Bake your brooch in the oven on a cookie tin for about 30 minutes at 265 degrees (follow the directions on the back of the clay package).

5 Let your brooch cool and glue on a pin back.

"To the victor goes the spoils"

money and gained political power by conquering new territories. You've probably heard the phrase, "To the victor goes the spoils." In this case it was very true. Money from selling slaves and raiding towns went right into the pockets of the consuls. But the consuls had to keep a careful balance. It was important that they didn't inflict too much damage to the communities they raided. If people in the new territories were too unhappy, they might become rebellious and make it difficult for Rome to rule them.

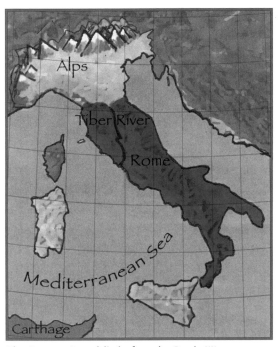

The Roman Republic before the Punic Wars.

A balance would also have to be struck between conquering more and more territory and then having the manpower—both the army and the administrators—to control the new lands. The system of setting up newly acquired territories as self-governing provinces who paid taxes to Rome in return for military protection worked pretty well until the Roman army became stretched so thin they couldn't offer the necessary protection.

The Punic Wars

Between 264 and 146 BCE, the Roman military fought the three Punic Wars against Carthage, a major city on the Mediterranean coast of Africa. For many years, Carthage was Rome's greatest rival on the Mediterranean Sea. The Carthaginians were fantastic sailors and controlled most of the sea trade and many of the islands in the Mediterranean. The Romans were fierce warriors and fantastic soldiers on land, but were not good sailors—all their conquests and trading was via land. The First Punic War (264–251 BCE)—fought throughout the Mediterranean Sea—lasted 13 years. The Romans had to learn how to build boats and then sail them, but they finally beat the Carthaginians. After this war, Rome controlled Sicily, Sardinia, and Corsica—all islands in the Mediterranean Sea that were previously under the control of Carthage.

Q: Who built the *Via Appia*? How long was it?

During the Second Punic War (218–202 BCE), the Romans fought against the Carthaginian general Hannibal, known as one of the greatest generals of all time. Spain had been defeated by Carthage in the 220s BCE, which allowed Hannibal and his army to go through Spain and across the Alps, approaching Italy by land from the north. Hannibal sent word ahead, hoping to get help from the Italian communities that had been conquered and annexed by Rome. Some communities—like Syracuse in Sicily and a few of the southern Italian cities—offered to help in Hannibal's attempt to defeat the Roman army, but most didn't want to get involved.

Although Hannibal had many victories, he struggled to win the war. Eventually Rome invaded Africa, and Hannibal headed back to help protect his homeland. He was defeated at Zama, near Carthage, in 202 BCE by the Roman general, Publius Cornelius Scipio. The victory earned Scipio the surname Africanus. He is known as Scipio Africanus the Elder. As part of a fifty-year negotiated peace, Carthage had to give all their colonies to Rome and pay the Romans a huge fine.

In 146 BCE, after the 50-year peace expired, Rome invaded Carthage again and destroyed it in what is known as the Third Punic War. Carthaginians who didn't die

The word *Punic* comes from the word *Phoenician*. The Carthaginians were a branch of the Phoenician family. The Romans used the term Punic to refer specifically to Carthaginians, the people who lived in Carthage.

Interesting Tidbit: *Punic*

Hannibal Crosses the Alps

When Hannibal set out from New Carthage, now Cartegena, Spain, to cross the Alps and enter Italy in 218 BCE, it was with a strange cast of characters. He brought elephants, possibly camels, Africans, Celts, Moors, Spaniards, and Carthaginians with him. Because of the terribly rugged terrain, Hannibal lost both people and animals while crossing the Alps—perhaps as many as half of the people and animals died—but Hannibal was relying on the element of surprise. When Hannibal met up with the Roman army commanded by Publius Cornelius Scipio at the River Trebia, he beat the Romans badly. Imagine being a Roman soldier in northern Italy and coming face to face with an African elephant!

in the war were sold into slavery. At war's end, the Roman army set the entire city of Carthage on fire and let it burn for 17 days. Then they knocked over anything that was left standing and, according to legend, plowed salt into the earth so that nothing would grow. Ever. They wanted no further trouble from Carthage.

To the East, in Greece

Meanwhile, to the east, the Romans fought war after war with Greece. Let's set the scene. After the Greek leader Alexander the Great died in 323 BCE, his empire was split between his generals. Three dynasties emerged—one in Macedonia, one in Asia Minor and the Near East, and one in Egypt. The Romans defeated armies in Macedonia and Asia Minor in the second century BCE but didn't annex the territories. They gave these territories a lot of freedom in governing themselves. Then the Romans found themselves fighting in Macedonia again just 30 years later. This time they seized Macedonia as a province, abolished the kingdom, and divided the territory into four republics.

The Beginning of the End

What did conquering all the land around the Mediterranean Sea mean for Rome? In a word, the beginning of the end. First, there weren't enough Roman administrators—or praetors—to oversee and manage the new territories or provinces. As happened with Macedonia, the Roman army found itself having to defend Roman rule in territories it had conquered just a few years earlier. This led to problems within the military, which had a hard time recruiting enough soldiers to fill the ranks. As the Roman empire got larger, the Roman army had to cover much more territory. By this time, the majority of the men serving in the army were from small farms. They joined the army because they weren't making any money on their farms. The small farms couldn't compete economically with the large estates, which were being run with slave labor. Imagine the problems this caused Rome, depending on an army made up of men forced off their land by rich landowners.

So, Rome looked beyond the small farmers to recruit new soldiers. Who did they turn to? Their Italian allies. Soon the allies were providing enough soldiers to make up about half of

Out of the Mouths of Romans

Cato the Elder

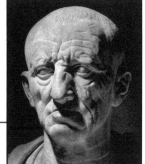

"It is my opinion that Carthage must be destroyed." Cato the Elder, a famous orator and member of the Senate in the 150s BCE, ended every single opinion he gave with this statement, whether or not it had anything to do with the discussion.

names *you should know*

Alexander the Great (356–323 BCE)

A great Macedonian king and brilliant military commander who conquered Egypt and Asia Minor for Greece before he died at the young age of 33.

Rome's army. At first Rome offered less pay to the Italian recruits than they offered Roman citizens who served in the army. But when the new soldiers found out they were receiving less pay for equal service, they were angry. They wanted the same level of pay that Roman citizens were paid, and all the rights of a Roman citizen. Rome found itself at a crossroads. They could make their allies—people who lived in the annexed territories and provinces—citizens of Rome, which would give them rights equal to other Roman citizens under the law, or they could ignore the situation. They chose to ignore the situation.

Q: Why was it *bad* for the Romans to *expand so much?*

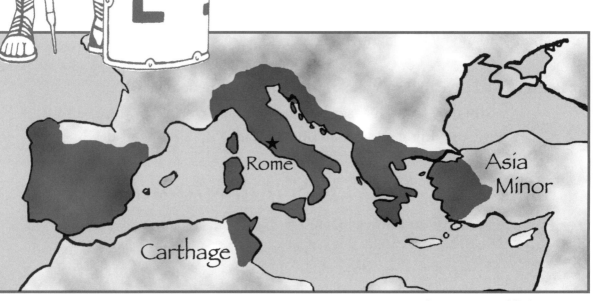

The Roman republic in 133 BCE.

CHAPTER

4

Witness the
senators'greed,
and fear of
the poor

See why
Caesar's life is
worthy of the
worldwide stage

Explore the
crafty mind of
Rome's first
emperor

The Demise of the Republic

IN 133 BCE, TIBERIUS SEMPRONIUS GRACCHUS, a tribune, introduced the idea of land reform to the Senate. He wanted to take public land that was being used by private individuals (often rich people who were farming the land to make even more money) and divide it into small parcels. These parcels would then be given to land-poor citizens in order to make them eligible for military service. Remember, Rome needed a large army to control its vast empire. A group of wealthy senators did not like Tiberius's idea at all, and when Tiberius tried to seek reelection, a mob of senators attacked and killed him and a number of his supporters.

Things just went downhill in the Roman Republic. A decade after Tiberius was killed, his brother Gaius,

Interesting Tidbit:
Nomenclator

A nomenclator was a slave with a very good memory. He went out in public with his master and told him the names of all the important people they were about to pass on the street. This way the master could seem very smart as he correctly addressed everyone by name.

also a tribune, proposed giving the right to vote to Italian allies. This made the poor of Rome angry because they feared what little power they had would be taken away by outsiders. The Senate didn't like Gaius because he was always proposing reforms that hurt the rich and helped the poor (like keeping grain prices low). So Senators did what they could to encourage the poor to dislike Gaius. After Gaius lost the election for tribune in 121 BCE as a result of the Senate manipulating the poor against him, he and his supporters staged a protest in the streets of Rome. Unfortunately, the protest got out of hand and became violent. The fact that some of Gaius's supporters were

Roman Names

Roman men usually had three names, and sometimes four. The first name was like our first name. Common first names were Gaius, Marcus, and Lucius. The second name was the clan name (a clan is a group of people who feel a connection to one another, usually through marriage). And the third name was the family name. So Tiberius Sempronius Gracchus would be a man named Tiberius from the Gracchus family of the Sempronius clan. One big problem in ancient Rome was that there could be many people with the same name. This was solved by getting a nickname. For example, Publius Cornelius Scipio became P. Cornelius Scipio Africanus after beating the Carthaginians at Zema, in northern Africa.

It was more difficult to figure out who was who among Roman women. Girls weren't given a first name. A girl was given the feminine form of her father's clan name plus the family name. It became really confusing if she had sisters because they all had the same name! How did outsiders distinguish one sister from another? If there were two sisters, the oldest would have *Maior* (major) after her name and the youngest would have *Minor*. If there were more than two sisters, they would be distinguished by numbers—*Prima, Secunda, Tertia* (first, second, third), and so on—until all the sisters were named. When a woman married, she took the feminine version of her husband's name. For example, Claudia Scipio Fundani was the daughter of somebody named Claudius Scipio and the wife of some guy named Fundanus.

armed gave the senators the excuse they needed to pass a decree allowing troops to attack Gaius and his supporters. After seeing the destruction around him and knowing he was going to be caught, Gaius committed suicide.

The Senate Loses Power

As distrust of the Senate grew among the common people, three things happened over the next few decades to further erode its power. First, due to a need for more soldiers, men who didn't own land were finally allowed to serve in the army—and they were even promised land at the end of their service. This seemed like a good idea and a way to get more soldiers into the military, but it would prove to be a big mistake for the state. The problem was that the state didn't distribute land to soldiers who completed their service. That task was left to the army commanders. The most successful military commanders were those who could promise the most land to their men, and this

Q: What did the Senate have against *Tiberius and his brother Gaius?*

names *you should know*

The Gracchus Brothers

The Gracchus brothers, Tiberius and Gaius, became heroes to the poor of Rome. They tried to enact reforms that gave public land to Roman citizens who were too poor to purchase land on their own. The Senators didn't like this idea because it threatened their financial advantage and power over the poor. Years after they died, statues of Tiberius and Gaius were erected on the spots where they died.

Lucius Cornelius Sulla (138–78 BCE)

Sulla was a consul who attacked the city of Rome when he didn't get his own way, and declared himself dictator.

made the soldiers more loyal to their commander than they were to the central government. Just imagine what would happen if one of those commanders wanted to challenge the power of the central government in Rome. Would the army follow him, or would they be loyal to the state?

Second, many Italian allies had finally had enough of being treated like second-class citizens and openly revolted against Rome. So Rome was having trouble with the military and trouble with their closest annexed neighbors.

Q: What made military leaders more powerful then the *central government?*

Then the inevitable happened. Lucius Cornelius Sulla, a consul and commander of an army, used troops loyal to him to take control of the city of Rome. He killed all his enemies and declared himself dictator. A dictator was like a king—he had all the power and could do as he wished. By declaring himself dictator, Sulla proved that a clever man could use the might of the military to gain political power for himself.

The Rise of Powerful Generals

The following three decades (78–49 BCE) were chaotic. Warlords emerged—generals who realized, like Sulla, that they could gain unprecedented powers through military threat. Gnaeus Pompeius Magnus, nicknamed Pompey, received a command in Spain by threatening the Senate. Then he was given command over the entire Mediterranean Sea.

The Senate gave him ships, money, and men to tackle the problem of piracy. There were so many pirates that sea trade on the Mediterranean had almost stopped. Pompey was a fierce warrior and smart general, and he got rid of the pirates in short order. Then he moved on with his army to Asia Minor where he annexed territory, called Syria, for Rome. When Pompey finally returned to Rome he was an extremely wealthy man. Remember, these military men reaped the spoils of war, taking whatever they could when they conquered new territory.

Pompey formed an alliance with two other powerful Roman generals, Gaius Julius Caesar and Marcus Licinius Crassus. Called the First Triumvirate, they agreed to help each other out politically. Pompey and Crassus served as consuls and voted themselves juicy commands of armies in Spain and Syria. Caesar went to Gaul (modern France), where he extended Roman rule far to the north. Caesar proved to be a great military leader. His army was extremely loyal to him because he was a very fair man, and it soon became clear that the army would follow him anywhere.

names *you should know*

Pompey [Gnaeus Pompeius Magnus] (106–48 BCE)

Pompey annexed Syria as a province and opened the way for Roman expansion to the east. In 60 BCE, Pompey formed a triumvirate of consuls (three rulers) with Caesar and Crassus and the three self-appointed rulers ruled Rome and its territories for several years. When Crassus died and Caesar left Rome, Pompey was left as sole consul. When Caesar came back with an army in 48 BCE, Pompey met him on the battlefield and was defeated. He fled to Egypt where he was stabbed to death.

Julius Caesar [Gaius Julius Caesar] (c. 100–44 BCE)

Julius Caesar was a clever politician and general who eventually became dictator of Rome. He was assassinated by some of his senators, on the Ides of March in 44 BCE. Today, we still rely on many aspects of the "Julian" calendar developed by Caesar in 46 BCE.

Marcus Licinius Crassus (115–53 BCE)

Crassus came to fame as the military leader who defeated Spartacus and the slave revolt. He joined Pompey and Caesar in forming a triumvirate to rule Rome in 60 BCE. Crassus was killed on a military campaign against the Parthians in Persia.

Crossing the Rubicon

As things were heating up in Rome, Caesar was stationed with a legion of troops in Ravenna in northern Italy. The Senate, which was controlled by Pompey at the time, told him to disband his army or risk being called an enemy of the state. Instead, in 50 BCE Caesar gathered his troops and stood on the northern bank of the Rubicon River, the small river that separated his province from that of Rome. According to the Roman historian, Suetonius, Caesar said, "Let us go where the omens of the Gods and the crimes of our enemies summon us! The die is now cast."

He crossed the Rubicon and made his way into Rome where a bloody civil war took place for the next three years.

Today, the term "crossing the Rubicon" is used whenever someone commits to a risky course of action.

"crossing the Rubicon"
commiting to a risky course of action

Crassus was killed in battle, which left Pompey and Caesar—two men who didn't like or trust each other—in power. When Caesar needed to be reelected consul to keep his power, Pompey was very clever. He became the leader of Caesar's opponents (those who had preferred Crassus before he was killed), which meant that Caesar would not have the votes he needed to get reelected. Caesar marched his army into Italy (remember he was annexing territory for Rome in France). He crossed the Rubicon River and met his opponents head on. The two sides battled for the next three years, and in 46 BCE, Caesar emerged the winner. He pardoned his enemies, many of whom then supported him. Although Caesar held elections to fill many of the traditional offices, he had grander ideas for his own future. In 44 BCE, he appointed himself dictator for life, giving himself the power of a king.

Out of the Mouths of Romans

Plutarch (46–119 CE)

"I came, I saw, I conquered."

According to Plutarch, the words by which Julius Caesar succinctly described one of his victories. In Latin the words are "veni, vidi, vici."

That would prove to be Caesar's biggest mistake. Sixty senators didn't like the direction Rome was going—they were afraid they were going to lose the power they had—and took matters into their own hands. They assassinated Caesar on March 15, 44 BCE.

After Julius Caesar

Many senators hoped for a full restoration of the republic after the death of Caesar but they hadn't counted on the power of Caesar's heir. Caesar had no children of his own so he had adopted his 19-year-old great nephew—Gaius Octavianus Thurnius, known as Octavian. It was not unusual for powerful men to adopt relatives or even non-relatives as a way of guaranteeing heirs (individuals who would inherit their wealth and power).

The name Caesar signifies a supreme ruler. The words Kaiser in German, tsar in Russian, and qaysar in Islamic countries, are all words for rulers in those countries.

Although Octavian was young he was shrewd. Seeing themselves losing power, some senators tried to keep Octavian from

The Ides of March

The Ides is simply a term from the Roman calendar for the fifteenth day of March, May, July, and October, and the thirteenth day of every other month. On the Ides of March in 44 BCE, just three days before he was to leave for a military campaign in Parthia (modern-day Iraq), Julius Caesar was stabbed to death by a group of senators. The Ides of March came to represent a day of bad luck—a day when everyone should take precautions to prevent unexpected harm coming to them.

"Friends, Romans, countrymen, lend me your ears"

From the play *Julius Caesar*, by William Shakespeare, the first line of a speech in which Mark Antony addresses the crowd at Caesar's funeral.

assuming control. Octavian turned toward other powerful men who could help him defy the will of the Senate. Mark Antony (Marcus Antonius), a consul, was the most notable of them. Antony, however, also longed for power and so at times found himself allied with Octavian and at other times at odds with him. At one point, Octavian, Antony, and another general, Marcus Aemilius Lepidus, formed an alliance and appointed themselves triumvirs (we're back to three rulers), each grabbing a share of the empire. Lepidus took control of Africa, Antony took over the east, and Octavian remained in Italy. Soon, Octavian forced Lepidus out of office, leaving only Antony to deal with.

In a twist worthy of a soap opera (or a Shakespearean play) Antony was married to Octavian's sister, but that didn't stop him from carrying on an affair with the Egyptian ruler, Cleopatra. He was so smitten with Cleopatra that he gave her and her children Roman territory. Octavian was furious about that, and required Roman cities under his control to swear an oath of personal loyalty to him as he prepared for war. In 32 BCE, his forces met Antony and Cleopatra's forces in western Greece. Antony was

A Cesarean section is the delivery of an infant by surgical removal through an abdominal incision. The operation is of ancient origin and the name comes from the legend that Julius Caesar was born in this fashion.

Out of the Mouths of Romans

William Shakespeare (1564–1616 CE)

"Et tu Brute?"

These are Caesar's famous last words, spoken to his friend Brutus, who had betrayed him. In English they mean, "And even you, Brutus?"

1,600 years after Caesar's murder took place, Shakespeare borrowed this line for his play, Julius Caesar.

activity:
Make a Roman Newspaper

Now it's your turn to be a star reporter. Create a newspaper with a dateline of
March 15, 44 BCE

Include the following in your paper: The major story of the day (hint: something happened to Julius Caesar), Entertainment, Sports, What's happening around the Empire, Houses for Sale, Weather, Fashion, Special Events, Death notices, Advice Column

1 Look at several newspapers and notice how they look. Where do the articles appear? What do headlines look like? How many columns are there? Where do you find ads? The appearance of the paper is called the layout.

2 Write your stories. Keep in mind that newspaper stories are often short and to the point. Just the facts.

3 If you have a computer, you can do the layout on the screen using columns. If you want to do it by hand, write or type your articles, making sure to make them look like a newspaper article.

4 Don't forget photographs or illustrations. And remember the captions underneath the pictures.

FINISHED PAPER

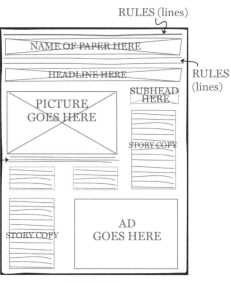

LAYOUT

names *you should know*

Cicero [Marcus Tullius Cicero] (106–43 BCE)

Cicero was a famous speaker and writer. Unfortunately, Cicero wanted Rome to be a republic once again and he made Mark Antony and Octavian mad by writing some nasty things about them. Antony and Octavian had Cicero put to death by having his head and hands cut off.

outmaneuvered by Octavian, and a year later he and Cleopatra fled to Egypt where they died. This left Octavian the only survivor of the triumvir, and the first thing he did as sole leader of Rome was make sure that no one would ever challenge him again.

Q: What kind of government replaced the *republic?*

Cleopatra, ruler of Egypt.

The End of the Republic

Throughout the last century of the Roman Republic, even while Rome expanded, the political system had been falling apart as the government became further and further out of touch with the most basic needs of the Roman people. The rich were growing richer, and the poor were growing poorer. By the end of the republic, in about 30 BCE, , this was a problem all over Roman territory. Senators were frequently reduced to violent power struggles, which tended to end in riots or murder. This civil unrest provided a golden opportunity for a brilliant leader, and Octavian was perfectly positioned to take advantage of the opportunity. He created an empire and closed the door on the republic forever.

Republic versus Empire

The Roman Republic refers to the period in Roman history from the time the last king ruled (remember Tarquin the Proud?) to the rise in power of Octavian. Throughout many of the years of the republic, the Senate and Assembly ruled (or at least the people they put in power ruled).

After Octavian came to power he changed his name to Augustus, and the Roman Empire began. This is when Rome, and the lands controlled by Rome, were ruled by one man, an emperor, sometimes self-appointed and other times named as a successor by a sitting emperor.

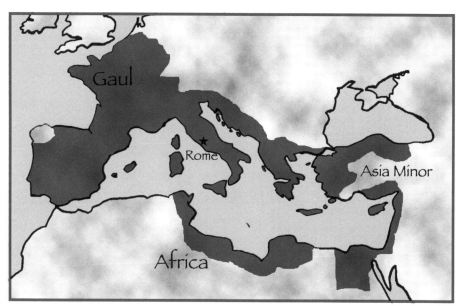

The Roman Republic in 30 BCE.

names *you should know*

Mark Antony [Marcus Antonius] (83–30 BCE)

A distinguished cavalry commander, Mark Antony is best known for his love affair with Cleopatra, the queen of Egypt. Unfortunately, Mark Antony was married to Octavian's sister when he took up with Cleopatra, which made Octavian very angry. Octavian defeated Antony and Cleopatra's military forces in 31 BCE and then chased the couple to Egypt where they both committed suicide.

activity: **Roman Medal**

Rome issued medals and coins to commemorate great deeds.

1 Use the serrated knife to carefully cut several Styrofoam cups about 1½ inches from the bottom. Keep the bottoms and throw away the tops.

about 1 ½ inches

2 Trace around the bottoms on a piece of paper. Now draw your design. Whatever you come up with will be the mirror image of what you'll get at the end so if you're using words, you have to write them backwards. Practice writing backwards by holding your words up to a mirror to check them.

3 Using your ballpoint pen, transfer your design to the bottom of the Styrofoam cup. Press hard so that your pen digs right into the Styrofoam and traces the outline.

Make a couple of medals at a time.

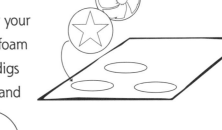

transfer design to bottom of cup

supplies

serrated knife
Styrofoam cups
paper
ballpoint pen
plaster of Paris
old coffee can
metal-colored paint
paintbrush

4 Mix up some plaster in the coffee can. Make sure the can is clean and dry before you start. You don't need much plaster—maybe mix up ½ cup of cold water to about ¾ cup of plaster—that should be plenty.

5 Carefully pour the plaster into the Styrofoam cup–until it's about ½ inch full–and let sit for at least 30 minutes.

6 Tear the Styrofoam away from the plaster and you'll see your medal!

7 Paint with the metal-colored paint to make the design stand out even more.

Discover how and why Roman roads were built so well

Find out how Roman arches, aqueducts, and bathhouses worked

Analyze the engineering secrets hehind Roman military success

Remarkable Feats in Engineering & Technology

THROUGHOUT THEIR LONG HISTORY, ROMANS BECAME known for their simple, durable buildings (like their many temples and the Coliseum), their public works projects (like aqueducts, sewers, and roads), and their military siege machines (such as catapults). All of these structures or creations showed a real aptitude for engineering. Once the Romans decided that something worked—either the designs or the materials they used—they stuck with it.

The Romans began working with concrete in about 300 BCE. They discovered that if they put the hard volcanic sand from

Mount Vesuvius into the mix, the concrete became very hard and able to withstand any kind of weather. This mixture was durable enough that they could even use it underwater.

Roads

Let's start with Roman roads. Under Gaius Gracchus, the Romans began building roads from Rome to various parts of the republic. As the republic grew, so did the length of the roads. Roads were originally built to enable the military to move quickly. Think about it, taking a road is a heck of a lot easier than bushwhacking through dense forest and marshland. Trade and commerce, and even communication between different parts of the republic grew with the development of the roads.

How do you make concrete?

First you heat limestone until all the water burns off. Then you pulverize what's left—the lime—and mix it with sand (in Rome's case, the sand from Mount Vesuvius). This is called mortar. Mix your mortar with small stones and gravel to get the concrete mix. Finally, add water, mix thoroughly, and let it set. Voilà. You've got concrete.

The Romans weren't the first to use concrete—the ancient Mesopotamians and the Egyptians used it as well. But as with many things the Romans did, they took an existing technology and improved it.

Roman roads were marked by mileposts measured from the *miliariaum aureum,* or the "golden milepost," which was a marker located in the Forum. This was the marketplace in the middle of the city of Rome. A Roman mile was measured at 1,000 paces. Our word mile comes from the Roman word for "thousand" *(mille).*

Once it was determined that a road should be built, the course of the road was very carefully laid out. The routes ran straight from one sighting point to another—no curves—or followed the natural topography of the land. All the material used in building roads was collected from the local area, since it didn't make sense to cart stones over long distances. The use of local materials meant that Roman roads were different throughout the republic.

Q: What are the origins of the *mile?*

The most important roads were called *viae publicae* (public roads), which were funded by the state. Next were *viae militares* (military roads), which were built at the expense of the army, but became public roads after they were built. Local roads were called *viae actus*. And finally there were *viae privatae* (private roads) built and maintained by the person who owned the road.

After figuring out the course of the road, it was time to build. First, the Romans built up an embankment, called an *agger*, for good drainage, which was very important if you wanted the road to last. Larger stones were laid at the base of this embankment to allow for drainage. Next came the middle layer of sand and gravel, sometimes mixed with clay, that made the road more durable. The sand and gravel would be well flattened, or tamped down. The top surface, called the *metalling* (although it was not made from metal), had to be hard to withstand the impact of weather and lots of use. On roads near cities the metalling surface was made up of flat stones, called paving stones. In the country, road

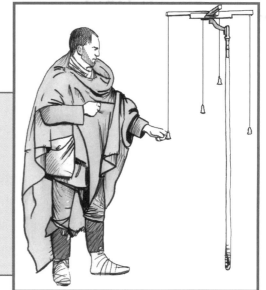

Surveying equipment

A *groma* was the main surveying instrument of Roman surveyors. It consisted of two crossed sticks attached to a vertical staff that was placed in the ground. From the end of each stick hung a string with a plumb bob, or weight, attached. Surveyors used a *groma* to determine straight lines and right angles.

A groma.,

builders used a fine dust and gravel, which hardened like cement over time.

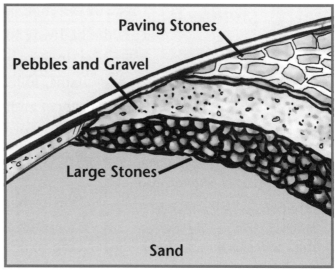

Paving Stones

Pebbles and Gravel

Large Stones

Sand

Road width varied from a maximum of about 40 feet on public roads, to a minimum of 8 feet on private roads. Sometimes, to help horse-drawn wagons through steep or slick parts of a road, tracks were cut lengthwise into a road to guide the wheels, and grooves were cut across a road to give a horse better footing.

The Romans built 50,000 miles of hard-surfaced roads, mostly for the military

Romans figured out how to build roads over extensive wetlands or swampy areas. First, they would drive wooden pilings into a marsh and build an elevated wooden platform (like a boardwalk). They'd build the road on top of this platform. Paving stones were placed on the platform and gravel and sand was laid on top of that.

If roads had to cross rivers, road builders built bridges by digging down to bedrock and cementing the foundations of the piers. Then, with the guidance of engineers, the laborers used stone arches to span the river to create a beautiful Roman bridge.

In a mountainous region, the Romans would try to follow the contours of the land when possible. Then, if they had to, they would cut roadbeds into the sides of mountains. On occasion, they even tunneled through. You can still see some Roman tunnels along the Via Flaminia and the Via Appia. Ultimately, Romans built about 50,000 miles of roads through their vast empire, linking the city of Rome to outposts as far away as Hadrian's Wall in Britain.

Out of the Mouths of Romans

Statius

In a poem by Statius, one of the premier poets of his time (45–96 CE), he explains the construction of a Roman road:

"The first task here is to trace furrows, ripping up the maze of paths, and then excavate a deep trench in the ground. The second comprises refilling the trench with other material to make a foundation for the road build-up. The ground must not give way nor must bedrock or base be at all unreliable when the paving stones are trodden. Next the road metalling is held in place on both sides by kerbing and numerous wedges. How numerous the squads working together! Some are cutting down woodland and clearing the higher ground, others are using tools to smooth outcrops of rock and plane great beams. There are those binding stones and consolidating the material with burnt lime and volcanic tufa. Others again are working hard to dry up hollows that keep filling with water or are diverting the smaller streams."

As with our modern roads, lots of businesses grew up along the highway to serve and profit from the many travelers. In Roman times these businesses included public baths, toilets, places to stay, shops, and the Roman version of fast-food joints.

Traffic became so congested in the city of Rome that Julius Caesar banned delivery traffic during the day (this would be similar to our truck traffic, only goods were moved by horse- or oxen-drawn carts). Although this helped clear up some of the clogged roads, it didn't make people who lived in the city very happy when they had to listen to delivery carts all night long!

Hadrian's Wall was built in 122 CE all the way across Britain to keep the barbarians from invading the Roman Empire. It was 12 feet high and 73 miles long

Aqueducts

Although aqueducts were not invented by the Romans, the Romans put aqueducts on the map.

What is an aqueduct? It's basically a manmade channel or pipe built to bring water to people where they live. The Roman aqueducts were often enclosed in large pipes, which ran through a series of tunnels and enclosed bridges. Water from a lake or other large catch-basin would flow through the aqueduct, downhill to the city, where it was collected in another large basin. From there, smaller pipes would siphon off the water and distribute it to public baths, fountains, and neighborhoods.

The first Roman aqueduct, *Aqua Appia*, was built in 312 BCE and was about 10 miles long. Over the next several hundred years, 10 more aqueducts were built to supply enough water for Rome's fountains and public baths.

Q: List the phases of construction in a *Roman Road*.

As with Roman roads, the building of aqueducts required a lot of planning and hard work. When planners identified a good source of water, such as a lake, they sent surveyors out to calculate the difference in elevation between the source and the water's destination in the city. Bodies of water were generally in the hills, higher up than the cities. Then they carefully planned a route to make sure there was a continuous, gentle, downhill grade, so the water could make use of gravity on its journey toward the city.

Most of the aqueducts ran underground so the water would stay cool. Often the aqueducts or pipes were buried in trenches, but sometimes,

Take to the Road

When the city of Pompeii was excavated, archeologists found something very interesting built right into the road—raised stepping stones so people could cross the street without having to step down onto the road. There were spaces between the stepping stones to allow the wheels of a cart or wagon to pass. There were also raised sidewalks lining the edges of the road. Although this is hard to imagine today, think about why you wouldn't want to be walking at road level (hint: think about what pulls wagons and what they leave behind).

Q. What is an *aqueduct?*

in order to continue the proper downhill gradient, deeper tunnels were dug. The aqueduct itself was a closed pipe that was as tall as a man so that someone could enter the aqueduct periodically to clean it.

If the pipe couldn't be buried underground, it was supported on road-like structures, or built into overpasses or bridges. The Romans created many beautiful bridges supported by arches to carry their aqueducts. The most famous Roman aqueduct still around today is probably the Pont du Gard in Provence, France, built by the Roman emperor Trajan in the first century CE.

Roman Baths

Almost every Roman city had at least one public bathhouse, or *thermae*. Everyone went to the baths—rich and poor, young and old, man and woman alike. Baths were not only a place to get clean, they were also meeting places and places of entertainment, something like the modern-day shopping mall.

The bathhouses were a series of rooms, with separate sections for men and women. The first room was the changing room (*apotyterium*), followed by a hot bath room (*caldarium*), then a warm bath or intermediate room (*tepidarium*), and, finally, the cold bath room (*frigidarium*). A swimming pool (*natatio*), saunas, libraries, gymnasiums, reading rooms, and lounges rounded out the bath complex.

Interesting Tidbit:
Water and the City of Rome

It's been calculated that between the third and fourth centuries CE, the city of Rome was provided with over three million cubic feet of water a day to meet the needs of a population of around one million. This means that ancient Romans were using twice as much water per person as modern Romans.

The baths got their water from pipes that ran from large cisterns fed by an aqueduct. Some water went directly into the cold baths. Water for the warm and hot baths was first diverted to the boilers, where it was heated. It was then mixed with cold water and sent through pipes to the *tepidarium* and the *caldarium*.

In some bathhouses, another method of heating the water also provided space-heating for the baths. A fire was lit in an oven and the hot air it created flowed through a space under the floor called the *hypocaust*. The heat then rose through a network of brick pipes that blanketed the walls of the *caldarium*, thoroughly heating the room. The floor of the *caldarium* was often too hot to walk on with bare feet so bathers wore wooden-soled clogs. This system of heating was also used in private villas.

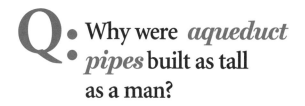

Q: Why were *aqueduct pipes* built as tall as a man?

Roman Architecture

The most distinctive element of Roman architecture is probably the arch. The Romans borrowed the idea for the arch from the Etruscans and improved upon it. Arches were found in bridges and aqueducts and were the basic support structure of many buildings.

Arch construction allowed the Romans to build very large

Interesting Tidbit:
Water, Water Everywhere

At its peak, the city of Rome had 11 huge public baths, 856 middle to small sized public baths, 15 monumental fountains, 1,352 smaller fountains and basins, and two *naumachiae* (where staged sea battles were held, which you'll read about later). All of this water was supplied by 11 aqueducts bringing water into the city.

structures, such as **amphitheaters**. An amphitheater is a huge oval building surrounding a flat, open area called an arena. The outside walls of amphitheaters were generally a series of arcades (connected arches) stacked one on top of the other. Because the arch distributes weight evenly but is relatively light, Roman builders could build high walls of stone without fear that the walls would collapse of their own weight. Today, the best-known example of a Roman amphitheater is the Coliseum in Rome.

Q. *What civilization* did the Romans model their *temples* after?

Other famous ancient Roman buildings are the temples. Roman temples looked a lot like Greek temples of the time. The Romans loved all things Greek, including their architecture. Conquering Greek territory and acquiring Greek slaves gave Romans access to Greek ideas and technology. Most Roman temples were large rectangular buildings with columns in the front that held up a pediment. However, the most famous Roman temple, called the Pantheon, is round.

Interesting Tidbit:
The Pantheon

"Pantheon" is the word for the entire collection of the Roman gods. The building called the Pantheon is a Roman temple dedicated to the gods.

The Arch

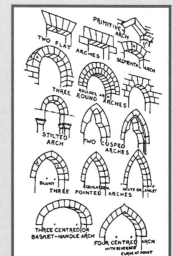

Although the Romans didn't invent the arch, they sure did perfect it. The Romans came up with the idea of using a keystone (also called a capstone or just the key). This is a V-shaped stone set at the top of the arch, which takes the weight from above and evenly distributes it down both sides of the arch. As the weight presses down on the arch, the stones are compressed, which makes the arch even stronger! The Roman arch could support more weight than earlier designs, allowing them to build bigger and bigger structures (like the Coliseum).

Have you ever tried to build an arch? It's impossible to keep the pieces together until you put in the keystone. The Romans used a wooden frame to support the tapered stone blocks that made up the sides of the arch until the keystone could be put in place.

Look around your neighborhood, particularly at the public buildings and bridges, and see if you can spot examples of a Roman arch. Then try to figure out if these arches are structural (are they holding something up?) or just for decoration.

The Pantheon was built in about 25 BCE by Marcus Vipsanius Agrippa, the faithful advisor to Augustus, the first Roman emperor. The huge temple has a magnificent domed roof made of cast concrete, which stands behind a rectangular, columned porch. The dome has a diameter of 143 feet and is still the largest dome ever made without using reinforced concrete. It has a 30-foot-wide circular opening—called an *oculus*—at the top of the dome to let in light. The height of the dome is 143 feet, equal to the diameter, making the Pantheon a perfect hemisphere (half-circle). The first Pantheon burned down and was rebuilt by Emperor Hadrian around 120 CE.

KNOW YOUR ROMAN *Architecture*

aqueduct: A channel or pipe that transports water.

Ampitheater: An oval building or arena for gladiator contests and other spectacles.

activity: **Roman Ruins**

This activitiy is a way to get familiar with parts of a Roman building. You'll make a column, a column base, and a pediment (the large triangular part of the building that's held up by the columns). If you're feeling ambitious, you can make an arch.

1 Take a bit of the clay in your hand and work it around so that it gets nice and soft. Roll it into a ball and then start to roll it on the work surface until you have a "column."

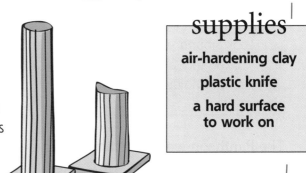

2 Cut the ends off your column, then make lines down the length of the column. Make several columns of different lengths.

3 Flatten some clay and cut pieces into squares with hollowed-out centers. Fit a couple of your columns into these—they're the base of the column.

4 Flatten some more clay and cut out a large triangle. This triangle represents a pediment— the large triangular part of the building that's held up by the columns.

5 Look at a picture of a Roman building and try to copy some of the details in clay. Can you figure out how to make an amphitheater?

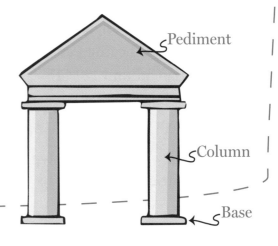

Pediment

Column

Base

Technology of War

As usual, the Romans borrowed and adapted much of their military technology from other cultures. They learned a great deal from the innovations of Archimedes, a Greek mathematician and engineer. Archimedes served as a military consultant to the Greeks during the Roman siege on the Greek city of Syracuse. He was killed during the sack of the city, which was very unfortunate for the field of technology (as well as math, physics, and philosophy).

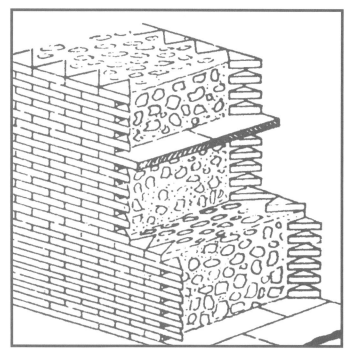

Assault tower.

Throughout ancient Roman history, Roman military forces were almost always fighting somewhere. They were either defending their hold on territory they'd already gained, or they were trying to expand Roman borders even further. One of the greatest challenges to expansion was taking over big cities. Unlike small towns, which usually didn't put up a fight, big cities were often defended by armies.

There were a couple of steps involved in laying siege to (or attacking) a city. First, the Romans surrounded the city with ditches and walls to keep anyone from getting in or out. Then, they figured out how to breach, or go over or through, the city walls. The main instrument used to breach walls were iron-tipped battering rams called aries and boring drills called terebras. These siege machines were often so heavy that they had to be rolled up to a wall.

Another tool Romans used against fortified cities was a huge assault tower on wheels. They built these towers higher than the wall so they could shoot arrows down into the city while they lowered a bridge onto the wall for their soldiers to enter the city

The catapult was an effective weapon in the capture of cities and territory. A few kinds of catapults were used by the Romans. The **ballista** was a huge crossbow that shot flaming arrows. The ballista could fire the arrows with deadly accuracy and in rapid succession. The **oneger** was a smaller catapult that could be moved around because it was mounted on wheels. It shot either single stones or bags of stones and had a range of about 1,400 feet. A larger version of the oneger did not have wheels but could hurl boulders as heavy as 60 pounds up to half a mile.

The Romans were very aggressive and determined in their sieges. One of the most famous sieges was of Herod's fortress in Israel, in 73 CE. This was the site of the last stand of Jewish rebels against Rome. Roman soldiers built a wall along the circumference of the hilltop fortress and waited for two years, trying to starve the rebels and their families out. Finally, the Romans built a huge earthen siege ramp against the wall. When they entered the city, most of the rebels and their families killed themselves so as not to be taken by the Romans.

KNOW YOUR ANCIENT ROMAN *Weapons*

aries:	iron-tipped battering rams used to breach walls.	**ballista:**	a huge crossbow that shot flaming arrows.
terebra:	giant drills that were rolled up to fortress walls.	**oneger:**	a small, easy-to-move catapult on wheels.

Birth of an Empire

WHEN OCTAVIAN TOOK CONTROL AFTER THE DEATH of Mark Antony in 32 BCE, he very carefully kept the appearance of maintaining a republic. He knew it was best to try to make the Senate and the people happy, as most of the rulers who hadn't done that ended up dead. The Senate gave Octavian the name "Augustus" in 27 BCE. *Augustus* means "Revered One." He also received the title *princeps*, or first citizen of Rome. The titles *Augustus* and *princeps* would be used by the rulers of the Roman empire until 293 CE.

names *you should know*

Augustus [Gaius Octavius] (63 BCE–14 CE)

Adopted by his uncle, Julius Caesar, he became heir to the Roman empire at the age of 18. Octavian (as he was then known) managed to win the support of the Senate and the people. He oversaw the massive expansion of the Roman Empire and, at the same time, he made many reforms for the betterment of Roman society. He was behind the construction of great temples like the Pantheon, public libraries, public baths, roads, aqueducts, and the first imperial Forum. He centralized the administration of the government and strengthened the borders of the empire, in part by paying the soldiers their back pay. Enormously wealthy, Augustus used his own money to promote economic stability, growth, and prosperity.

Out of the Mouths of Romans

Dio Cassius, Roman administrator and historian, author of a history of Rome

"The name Augustus was bestowed upon him by the Senate and the people. They wanted to address him by some special name, and while they were proposing one name or another, and deciding on it, Caesar [Octavian] was extremely eager to be called Romulus. When he perceived, however, that people therefore suspected him of yearning for a position as king, he no longer sought this title, but instead accepted the title Augustus, as if he were somewhat more than human; for everything that is most valuable and most sacred is called augustus."

The time period known as the Augustan Age goes from the death of Julius Caesar in 44 BCE to the death of the poet Ovid in 17 CE. Augustus ruled the Roman Empire from 29 BCE until his death in 14 CE—over four decades!

Over the course of Augustus's long rule, he came to embody and symbolize Rome. When he began his rule, things were a mess. The republic was financially bankrupt, struggling to maintain authority over the military (whose soldiers had not been paid for a while), and there was no stable central administration to look after the far-flung provinces. Augustus took control of the provinces and the armies. A very wealthy man, he was able to use his own money to straighten out the state and military. He developed an important system of administration so the far-off governments of the provinces had to report to the central government in Rome. That way he had more control over all the territory ruled by Rome.

Socially and culturally, Augustus promoted "traditional values." He instituted morality laws and provided rewards for marriage and children. He promoted religion and the importance of being a good citizen.

Great building and public works projects were begun under Augustus, including the Forum, temples, libraries, baths, the Mausoleum of Augustus, aqueducts, and roads. He knew that if Rome looked like an important imperial city, chances were good that it would act like one and be respected as one.

Unlike his predecessors, Augustus worked at strengthening the borders of the empire rather than expanding them. He also encouraged the provinces to become more economically stable and independent. Rome was very fortunate to have a man like Augustus as its first emperor. At his death in 14 CE, he left behind a prosperous empire very different from the unruly one he inherited 40 years before.

activity:
Map of the Roman Empire

The Roman Empire expanded and contracted over the centuries. Make a map and follow the changes!

1 Make a map of the region controlled by Rome in 100 BCE, 30 BCE, 150 CE, and 300 CE. Label both the Roman and modern names of the regions on your map.

2 Go to http://www.roman-empire.net/maps/map-empire.html and you will find maps from different eras. You can use the information you find here for your maps.

supplies

poster paper
markers

Praetorian Guards

Praetoriean Guards were the elite soldiers who originally surrounded and protected Roman generals. Augustus created several groups of elite bodyguards and called them the Royal Praetorian Guards. They were a force to be reckoned with, and they knew everything that was happening around the emperor. Throughout their history, they were at the center of a lot of palace plots and schemes.

Interesting Tidbit:
The Golden Age of Literature

Literature and art flourished under Augustus. Three of the most famous poets who ever lived— Ovid, Horace, and Virgil—wrote during the reign of Augustus.

A major difference between the Roman Republic and the Roman Empire was how the rulers were chosen. Remember, the republic was ruled jointly by two elected consuls, so the people had a say in who ruled them. The empire was ruled by an emperor, who the people had nothing to do with choosing.

Augustus became obsessed with who would succeed him as emperor. Tiberius (emperor from 14 BCE to 37 CE) was the son of Augustus's second wife, Livia. Augustus thought Tiberius would be a good emperor, so he convinced Tiberius to divorce his wife and marry his own step-sister, Augustus's daughter, Julia. Twenty-five years later Augustus adopted Tiberius to ensure an heir. When Augustus died, Tiberius was 56 and a well-trained general and administrator. During his rule he reduced taxes, built roads and other public works, and took care of the provinces. When Tiberius died, Rome was a much better place economically than it had been when he became emperor. Tiberius' greatest problem was that he wasn't a good people-person and didn't know how to be diplomatic. He struggled to get along with the Senate and many members of his own family. He eventually went to live in Capri and ruled the empire from afar. When he knew he was dying, he tried to return to Rome to ensure a smooth succession, but the prefect of the Praetorian Guard—a powerful and influential person who was supposed to protect the emperor's interests—suffocated him.

Mausoleum of Augustus (Mausoleum Divi Augusti). Drawing by Etienne Du Pérac from 1575

names *you should know*

Ovid [Publius Ovidius Naso] (43 BCE–17 CE)

Ovid was one of the greatest poets of antiquity and the author of *Metamorphoses*, a single epic poem containing several individual stories.

Caligula, the son of Tiberius's nephew, Germanicus, became emperor after Tiberius died. His real name was Gaius. Caligula was a nickname meaning "little boots" that was given to him as a young boy when he accompanied his father on military campaigns. While on these campaigns, Caligula was often dressed in miniature military clothing. Caligula became extremely ill during his first year as emperor, and when he recovered he was a changed man. He became a megalomaniac (someone who had to be in complete control of everything) who did outrageous things like appoint his favorite horse, Incitatus, to a seat in the Senate. Caligula disliked senators, and in one famous story had a group of them wait on him like slaves. He continued to do outrageous things, such as spending all of Rome's money in four short years, leading the military out on campaigns but then unexpectedly turning around and heading home, and even killing members of his own family. Finally, in an act all too familiar in Roman history, a member of the Praetorian Guard killed him in 41 CE.

Tiberius

Q. Why did *Octavian decide* not to adopt the title, *"Romulus,"* as he desired?

The next emperor was Claudius. He was Caligula's uncle and, according to the Roman historian Suetonius, was proclaimed emperor while hiding behind a curtain after Caligula was killed. There's a great deal we don't know about Claudius. Roman historians, like Suetonius, generally portray him as an idiot who was brought to power because he could be easily controlled by others. However, when you examine his record, it seems he was actually quite clever.

Who's Who in the Julio-Claudian Dynasty

The first of the Julio-Claudian emperors was Julius Caesar. He was succeeded by his nephew Octavian who renamed himself Augustus. Augustus named his stepson, Tiberius, (who was also married to his daughter) as his successor. Tiberius's grandnephew, Caligula, was named as successor to Tiberius. Claudius, Caligula's uncle, succeeded Caligula. Claudius married his niece, Agrippina (Caligula's sister) and adopted her son, Nero. Claudius conveniently died (some say poisoned by mushrooms given to him by Agrippina) just as Nero was old enough to assume power.

Out of the Mouths of Romans

What one Roman Historian thought of Octavian

"When he had seduced the military with gifts, the people with food, and all with sweet tranquility, he gradually usurped the powers of the Senate, magistrates, and courts. No real opposition remained—the bravest men were casualties of battle and proscriptions. He elevated the remaining nobility financially and politically according to their willingness to serve him and they, enriched by his regime, preferred the safety of their new arrangement to the dangers of the old. Nor did the provinces object: competition and greed of the wealthy and the governors had undermined the republic's legitimacy; power, favoritism, and primarily money had rendered the laws no help whatsoever."

Although he had a birth defect that left him deformed and with a speech impediment, Augustus, his grandfather, had recognized something special in him when he was young and had him tutored. Claudius was an expert on Roman law, history, and languages (Etruscan and Carthaginian). However, he had no administrative or military experience before coming to power.

Luckily, Claudius was smart enough to surround himself with very talented and ambitious freedmen. Freedmen, or freed slaves, had become very important to the government, because they were often placed in charge of imperial correspondence, records, and accounting. They had the power to bring matters before the emperor and to assist in the smooth running of the bureaucracy. Remember, slaves were taken from all over the empire and some were highly educated and talented men.

The empire's borders expanded under Claudius— he added Britain, Thrace, and Mauritania (in northwestern Africa). He also completed some great building projects, such as an artificial harbor at Ostia on the Tiber River. The empire was thriving.

names *you should know*

Livy [Titus Livius] (59 BCE to 17 CE)

A Roman historian from Padua, Livy wrote a 142-book history of Rome from its origins to 9 BCE.

But for all Claudius's public success, his private life was a wreck. After several messy marriages, he had the law changed so he could marry Caligula's sister, his niece, Agrippina. He adopted Agrippina's son, who was renamed Nero, and had him educated by the philosopher Seneca. When Nero turned 16 in 54 CE and was old enough to take power as emperor, Claudius mysteriously died.

Nero (emperor from 54 to 68 CE), his mother, and his mother's trusted advisors took over. Things went pretty well in the empire for several years, but eventually Nero found himself in a power struggle with his mother. At one point, he sent her out to sea in a boat that was rigged to sink, but she swam back to shore. Later, Nero sent some men to kill her. As the story goes, her last words were, "Strike here!" as she pointed to her womb, where she carried Nero for nine months of pregnancy.

Nero proved to be a terrible emperor. He insisted on participating in chariot races and performing on the stage, which greatly embarrassed the senators. They grew to hate him and his ego. Nero's personal life was also a mess. He was married several

names *you should know*

Seneca [Lucius Annaeus Seneca] (4 BCE–65 CE)

Seneca was a Spanish-born orator, best known as tutor and later political advisor to Nero.

Out of the Mouths of Romans

Tacitus on Nero

"But the terrible rumor that Nero himself had ordered the burning of Rome could not be quelled by charitable distributions or donations by the princes of ceremonies of atonement. Therefore Nero sought to put down the rumor by providing culprits and visited with outrageous punishments a group called Christians by the mob and hated for their misdeeds . . . So they first arrested professing Christians, then on their evidence a huge multitude who were convicted not so much on the charge of incendiarism as of hatred of the human race."

times and killed most of his wives. It was said that he roamed the streets in disguise so he could rob and assault people.

In 64 CE much of the city of Rome burned in a fire that raged for three days. It was well known that Nero wanted to build a palace in the area where the fire started. This raised suspicion that Nero had the fire set deliberately. Nero wasn't in the city when the fire started, and he rushed back to Rome to help the victims of the fire. When the rumors that Nero was behind the blaze didn't stop, Nero blamed the Christians for the fire. The fire cost the empire dearly. Money was needed to rebuild, and so the people were taxed. Nero took the opportunity to construct some public buildings and a huge imperial residence named the Golden House in the area that had burned. In 68 CE when civil and military unrest in Gaul and Spain threw Rome into chaos, the Senate declared Nero a public enemy. His days were numbered.

Q: Who did *Nero blame* for the fire of 64 CE?

Roman Society— Everyday Life

TODAY, YOUR DAILY LIFE VARIES DEPENDING ON WHERE you live. If you live on a farm, you have different chores than if you live in a city apartment. Also, your social life will vary according to where you live. People who live in cities and towns can probably walk or take a bus or subway to stores and movies, whereas people in rural areas might have to travel farther and use private modes of transportation.

Now, think about your daily life versus that of someone who lived 100, 200, or even 500 years ago. Now, transport yourself back to ancient Rome. Ancient Rome lasted from the seventh century BCE to at least the fourth century CE. That's over a thousand years! Let's look at everyday life during the late republic and early empire—when Roman influence was at its peak.

On the Farm

Life on a farm in ancient Rome varied depending on whether you were rich or poor. Wealthy landowners lived in big villas on large estates, and the work was done by slaves. Or, they lived in big houses in Rome and their estates were overseen by managers.

Most rural people, however, were poor. They owned small farms, between two and five acres in size, and worked very long hours for very little return. Every person in the family worked on the farm. The typical farmer grew grains to make flour for bread, and fruits and vegetables like carrots, radishes, cabbage, beans, beets, lentils, peas, onions, grapes, plums, pears, and apricots. They might also have a grove of olive trees. Most of the olives were eaten, but some were pressed to make olive oil to use for cooking or lamp-light. If a farmer had any extra grain he would sell it to a bakery.

By the early years of the empire, many small farmers had been forced off their land. The small farmers could not compete with the large estates worked by slaves that covered hundreds or even thousands of acres. Not having to pay the workers, large estates could produce things like grain or livestock very cheaply. As a result, many farmers lost their land when they couldn't pay their taxes. What happened to them? Many became tenant farmers and worked portions of the big estates in return for some of the harvest. Others left the land altogether and went to the city to look for work. Some were able to hold on to their land by going into the military, leaving wives and children at home to do all the work.

Q: Why couldn't people survive on *small farms?*

In the Cities and Towns

If you lived in a city, life was bustling. The cities were very cosmopolitan. People from all over the empire—Greeks, Romans, Orientals, Gauls, and Egyptians—mingled on the streets, in the shops, and in the taverns.

People traveled about the city on foot, by horse-drawn carts, or on palanquins—enclosed couches for one person, carried by several men. The streets were very crowded, and at night, because there was no public lighting, people had to carry lamps wherever they went.

Roman ruins.

The streets were lined with vendors and stores. It was possible to find anything and everything for sale in Rome—food, clothing, fabric, dishes, and art objects from around the world. Rome had bakeries, tanneries, artisan workshops, and banks. There were numerous building projects underway at any one time, bringing jobs, excitement, and noise to an already bustling city.

In the middle of most Roman towns was a forum, or public square. The forum was surrounded by public buildings and little shops—kind of like an outdoor pedestrian mall. This was the gathering place of the people, and also the place to conduct formal business. A temple usually stood at one end, and the basilica—the building that housed the city's commercial and public activities—ran along one side. The curia, the workplace of the municipal

activity: **Clay vessel**

The Romans stored oil and wine in clay vessels called amphora, *and made dishes and pots out of clay. They used a coil technique when making pottery.*

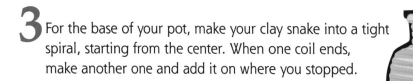

1 Take a clump of clay and work it in your hands to soften it. Start with a very small pot—maybe 3 inches tall— to get the hang of what you're doing.

2 Roll the clay into long "snakes" or coils—that's what you're going to use to make your pot. Make sure the coils are about the same size around from end to end.

3 For the base of your pot, make your clay snake into a tight spiral, starting from the center. When one coil ends, make another one and add it on where you stopped.

4 Build the pot by layering coils in the general shape you want your pot to be. Wet your fingers in the water and begin to smooth the clay on both the outside and the inside of the pot. Your coils will start to disappear. Refine the shape and continue smoothing over the clay with water.

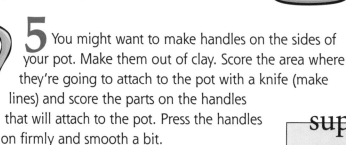

5 You might want to make handles on the sides of your pot. Make them out of clay. Score the area where they're going to attach to the pot with a knife (make lines) and score the parts on the handles that will attach to the pot. Press the handles on firmly and smooth a bit.

6 Let your pot air dry.

supplies

air-hardening clay
or
paperclay

a little bowl of water

Roman Numerals

The following letters of the Roman alphabet correspond with the following numbers:

I = 1	V = 5	X = 10
L = 50	C = 100	D = 500
M = 1000		

All other numbers are represented by a combination of letters. For example: III = 3 (1 + 1 + 1); XX = 20 (10 + 10); XIII = 13 (10 + 1 + 1 + 1); LXXIII = 73 (50 + 10 + 10 + 1 + 1 + 1).

The rule is to use the biggest numeral possible at each stage, so 15 would be XV and not VVV or XIIIII. You always read the numerals from left to right. Eventually a rule developed that allowed you to put a smaller value numeral to the left of a larger one that let you write a number in a kind of shorthand. For example, 4 could be written IV (1 less than 5) instead of IIII, or 90 could be written XC (10 less than 100) instead of LXXXX. Only the numerals I, X, and C can be used this way and you can only use one numeral this way at a time (you can't write 18 as IIXX). One final rule, the subtracted number to the left must be more than a tenth of the value of the number it's subtracted from. For example, 49 is XLIX (10 less than 50 plus 9) and not IL (1 less than 50).

Can you figure out how to write the number 1,999? MM would be the number 2,000. There are several answers, but one way to write 1,999 is MCMXCIX. Here's how you figure it out:

"M" represents 1,000; "CM" stands for 1,000 minus 100 (900); "XC" means 100 minus 10 (90); and "IX" is 10 minus 1 (9). 1,000 + 900 + 90 + 9 = 1,999. Phew.

Romans used a counting board or an abacus to do calculations.

I	1	XXI	21	XLI	41	LXI	61	LXXXI	81
II	2	XXII	22	XLII	42	LXII	62	LXXXII	82
III	3	XXIII	23	XLIII	43	LXIII	63	LXXXIII	83
IV	4	XXIV	24	XLIV	44	LXIV	64	LXXXIV	84
V	5	XXV	25	XLV	45	LXV	65	LXXXV	85
VI	6	XXVI	26	XLVI	46	LXVI	66	LXXXVI	86
VII	7	XXVII	27	XLVII	47	LXVII	67	LXXXVII	87
VIII	8	XXVIII	28	XLVIII	48	LXVIII	68	LXXXVIII	88
IX	9	XXIX	29	XLIX	49	LXIX	69	LXXXIX	89
X	10	XXX	30	L	50	LXX	70	XC	90
XI	11	XXXI	31	LI	51	LXXI	71	XCI	91
XII	12	XXXII	32	LII	52	LXXII	72	XCII	92
XIII	13	XXXIII	33	LIII	53	LXXIII	73	XCIII	93
XIV	14	XXXIV	34	LIV	54	LXXIV	74	XCIV	94
XV	15	XXXV	35	LV	55	LXXV	75	XCV	95
XVI	16	XXXVI	36	LVI	56	LXXVI	76	XCVI	96
XVII	17	XXXVII	37	LVII	57	LXXVII	77	XCVII	97
XVIII	18	XXXVIII	38	LVIII	58	LXXVIII	78	XCVIII	98
XIX	19	XXXIX	39	LIX	59	LXXIX	79	XCIX	99
XX	20	XL	40	LX	60	LXXX	80	C	100
								D	500
								M	1000

magistrates responsible for running the city, was another important building on the forum. There would also be a fountain and statues. And every town had a public bath, which was important not only for bathing but for socializing.

Homes

Most people lived in apartments or rooms in large blocks called *insulae* (which means "little island"). These buildings could be up to six stories tall. On the first floor would be shops and food stalls, and in nicer *insulae* there might be an inner courtyard with gardens, walkways, and fountains. As you went up in the *insulae* the rooms got smaller. The poorest people lived on the top floor. *Insulae* were notorious fire hazards because they were timber-framed buildings with mortar and rubble infill. That meant that if a fire started, it would go right up through the walls and travel from floor to floor. The buildings were also prone to collapse. After that big fire in Rome in 64 CE (that was rumored to be the work of Nero), certain building codes and restrictions were put in place, but they were not always observed.

A townhouse, where wealthier Romans lived, was called a *domus*. These townhouses often had a courtyard, gardens, an atrium (an enclosed garden space), dining room, kitchen, slave's room, and bedrooms.

Family

Within the Roman family, the father, or paterfamilias, had absolute power. He controlled all the property and made all the decisions. He decided when his children married and who they married. He also decided if marriages should end in divorce. He chose the careers of his sons. He even had the

Out of the Mouths of Romans

Seneca on Roman Baths

"I live over the public baths—you know what that means. Ugh! It's sickening. First there are the 'strongmen' doing their exercises and swinging heavy lead weights about with grunts and groans. Next the lazy ones having a cheap massage—I can hear someone being slapped on the shoulders. Then there's the man who always likes the sound of his own voice in the bath. And what about the ones who leap into the pool making a huge splash!"

power to decide if a member of his family should live or die when they did something improper. The father could punish a family member with banishment, slavery, or even death.

As discussed in chapter 2, the wife of the paterfamilias, called the materfamilias, was in charge of the household chores. She was also in charge of her children's education, and, when necessary, worked outside the home to help support the family. They were spinners, weavers, secretaries, shopkeepers, butchers, fishers, midwives, waitresses, and entertainers. Sometimes they were even physicians, landladies, moneylenders, businesswomen, or construction workers.

Boys were valued more highly than girls in ancient Rome (remember that girls didn't even have first names). The reason for this was that girls usually weren't allowed to do anything beyond what

Money in Ancient Rome

Ancient Rome used three coins: the *as*—a bronze coin, the *sestertius*—a small silver coin, and the *denarius*—a large silver coin (plural: *denarii*).

In 301 CE, sewer cleaners and day laborers were paid 25 *denarii* a day, the same amount a scribe would earn for copying 100 lines of script. Carpenters and bakers earned 60 *denarii* a day. A pound of pork cost 12 *denarii*. An arithmetic teacher earned about 2.5 *denarii* per student per day whereas a teacher of rhetoric or public speaking earned about 8 *denarii* per student per day. So if a sewer cleaner worked all day or a rhetoric teacher had three students, they earned enough to buy two pounds of pork.

During the time of Julius Caesar (around 50 BCE), a lot of the wealth was concentrated in the hands of very few people. Most people could only afford basic necessities. For example, a soldier was paid about 900 *sestertii* per year and a laborer earned about 1,000 *sestertii* per year. A senator, on the other hand, would have property valued at 800,000 *sestertii* (and many were considerably wealthier).

activity: **Abacus**

The Romans often used an abacus—a counter—to do arithmetic problems.

1 Cut a rectangle from the foam-board that measures 13 by 9 inches. USE YOUR XACTO KNIFE WITH CAUTION.

9 inches

13 inches

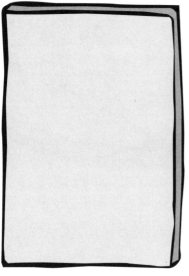

2 Cut six strips of foamboard—each 1 by 9 inches.

Glue two strips at each end of base

3 Glue two strips onto each of the short ends of the rectangle (you're building up a frame at the top and bottom).

supplies

foamboard
(about ¼ inch thick)

tape, glue, ruler

Xacto knife

bamboo skewers

60 craft beads in 2 colors *(30 beads each)*

pen, scissors

4 Take six bamboo skewers and place 10 beads on each—5 beads of one color on the bottom of each skewer and 5 beads of the other color on the top.

Tape ends down

5 Lay the beaded skewers lengthwise on the frame, and then tape the ends down onto the frame.

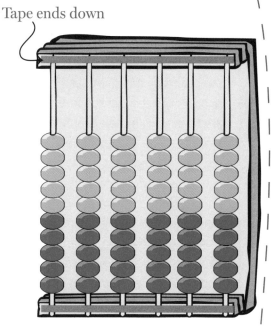

6 Put glue on the frame and then place the remaining strips of foamboard down to cover the ends of the bamboo skewers. Let the glue dry.

Secure each end with tape

7 Put a couple of pieces of tape on the ends to secure the frame.

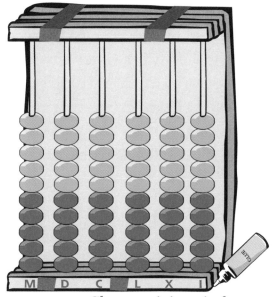

Glue remaining 1 inch strips over ends of skewers

8 Each row contains 10 beads worth one of the six basic Roman numerals. Label the bottom of your abacus from left to right: M, D, C, L, X, I. Lay your abacus flat. Now you can add and subtract by sliding the beads up and down.

M = 1000 L = 50
D = 500   X = 10
C = 100   I = 1

Martial, Roman poet, on life in Rome

"The schoolmasters won't leave you in peace in the morning or the bakers by night, and at all hours of the day the coppersmiths are beating with their hammers. Here, there's a moneychanger who, having nothing else to do, overturns a pile of coins on his filthy table; over there is a work-man with a gleaming hammer beating gold ore from Spain, already smashed into pieces . . . and who can tell how many hands beat copper receptacles in the city when, during an eclipse of the moon, spells are cast and magic rites practiced?"

was necessary to keep the family and home running smoothly, whereas boys had more potential to bring their family wealth or glory through military service, politics, or business.

Few Roman children went to school. They were taught at home by their parents, usually their mother. They learned Roman virtues like truthfulness, self-reliance, **piety**, respect for law, and obedience to authority. Boys from noble families might go to school or be tutored. Above all, they would be expected to master the art of public speaking, an important skill for boys headed for the Senate. Poor children went to work.

Health

While life in Rome was dangerous because of fires, collapsing buildings, and muggings, the real hazards lay in the area of public health. Chances of catching an easily spread disease were pretty good because, in addition to the city being very crowded, most people used the public baths. In the year 65 CE, 30,000 people died of the plague. If the **plague** didn't get you, an illness like **malaria** might. Today we know how diseases are spread, and we know how to treat and control them, but that wasn't the case in ancient Roman times.

words *to know*

piety: loyalty to parents and family.	**malaria:** a contagious disease in humid climates with chills and fever.
plague: a contagious disease that kills a lot of people who get it.	**malnutrition:** an inadequate or unbalanced diet that causes ill health.

Malnutrition was also a common problem until 123 BCE when a food law was enacted to help the poor. The state bought up grain in bulk and stored it in public warehouses, then sold a monthly ration to poor Roman citizens at a reduced price. With this system in place, Romans got used to a guaranteed food supply.

Interesting Tidbit:
The Orator

Being a good orator, or public speaker, was a very important skill to have in ancient Rome. The most effective senators were skilled orators. We might think of orators as being people who are good at arguing, but it was more than that. Orators had to be gifted and skilled in the art of delivering a persuasive argument. The point was to get people not only to listen to you, but also to agree with you.

Art

Art was highly valued in Roman culture, and beautiful art could be found throughout the homes of the wealthy. Mosaics (pictures made from tiny pieces of colored tile, stones, or beads) adorned walls and floors, with flowers, animals, hunting scenes—you name it! Some walls were decorated with frescoes, paintings done on wet plaster. Frescoes might depict landscapes or other scenes.

Statues were very popular and were found in temples, public places, and in homes. Statues and busts (just the head and shoulders) of the emperors were made and sent all over the empire. In the days before television and newspapers, this was one way the emperor could make sure his subjects knew who he was!

Wealthy Romans admired Greek statues and wanted them for their homes and gardens. Eventually, Roman art studios began to copy and sell them.

Out of the Mouths of Romans

Pliny the Elder

"Medicine is the only profession, by Jove, where any man off the street gains our immediate trust if he professes to be a doctor; and yet surely no lie would be more dangerous. But we don't worry about that; each one of us is lulled by the sweet hope of being healed. And we don't even have laws against the ignorance which endangers our lives.

activity: **Mosaic**

Mosaics were common throughout the Roman empire. Pictures on walls and floors were often created out of these little tiles (called tessera).

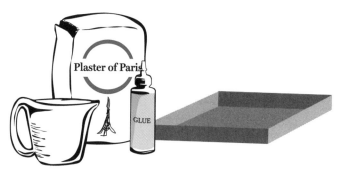

1 Mix up enough plaster to fill the reusable mosaic form (you can use an aluminum pie plate as well, although a square is easier to work with).

2 Pour plaster into the form, and let it sit until dry (at least 45 minutes).

3 Arrange your tiles on the table in the design you want to make. Don't place the tiles right next to each other because you need room to put the grout in. If you're doing a picture of an object, it often works best to make the design in the middle first, then fill in the tiles around the outside.

4 When the plaster is dry, remove it from the form.

supplies

reusable plastic mosaic form
or
an aluminum pan
(usually about 6 inches square)

plaster of Paris

little tiles
(sold in canisters in craft stores)

glue
(Elmer's is fine)

grout

plastic spatula

sponge

5 Transfer the tiles, one by one, to the surface of the plaster, placing a bit of glue on the back of each tile.

6 Let your design sit for a while to dry.

7 Mix up the grout with water until it becomes a thick paste.

8 Using the spatula, cover your mosaic with the grout, being sure to push it into the cracks. Don't worry that it's covering your design.

9 After the grout is covering the tiles, let it sit for a couple of minutes, then take a damp sponge and start to wipe it off the surface. Keep wiping until your tiles show and the extra grout is removed.

10 Let dry.

Glue tiles in a pattern on the plaster

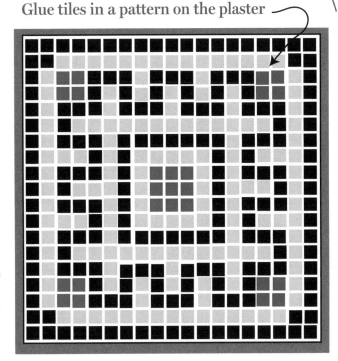

Interesting Tidbit:
Statues

Although Romans admired Greek statues, there was a big difference in their statues. The Greeks created idealized (or perfect) human forms in their statues, whereas the Romans created statues to resemble the people they were representing. In other words, if someone had a really big nose, a Greek sculptor would not carve the face the way it really existed, but the Roman sculptor would.

Some of the Greek statues we're familiar with today might not actually be originals, but Roman copies.

Friezes—scenes carved in stone—were very popular on public buildings and are a great way for us to get a glimpse into life in ancient Rome. Trajan's Column shows scenes of a victorious battle. In a long, spiral frieze on Augustus's Altar of Peace, there is a realistic scene showing members of his family and court taking part in a religious procession. From these friezes we can see details of everyday life—such as what people wore, and even what their hairstyles looked like.

Literature

Plautus and Terence, both playwrights, lived in the second century BCE (the 100s) and were the earliest Roman comedians. Much of the dialogue in their plays was recited to music or sung while actors danced.

Cicero (106–43 BCE) was the most famous literary figure of his time. Many of Cicero's written works survive, but he is best known as a

The Roman Calendar

The first day of the month was called the *calends* and the middle of the month was called the *ides* (from an Etruscan word that means divide). Priests determined whether it was going to be a long month or a short month by telling people when the *nonae* was going to fall—it was always nine days before the *ides* so it would either be on the fifth or the seventh day of the month.

The day after the *calends*, the *nonae*, and the *ides* were all called *nefasti* (ill-omened) and it was forbidden to do any business on these days. The Roman calendar didn't have weekends, so this gave people a couple of days off a month. The idea of a "week" as we know it didn't exist.

The early Romans had a 12-month, 355-day year, but the lunar month and the solar year were always getting out of step with each other, so the Romans had to add an extra month every other year.

By the time of Julius Caesar, the calendar was off by a whole season! He hired a Greek astronomer, Sosigenes, to straighten it out. Sosigenes suggested a year of 365.25 days. Caesar tried to fix everything in 46 BCE by adding an extra 67 days, plus an additional month of 23 days at the end of the year. He also suggested that each year should be 365 days long with an additional day added every fourth year—the leap year.

The priests misinterpreted Caesar's leap year and added an extra day every three years, which Augustus straightened out during his reign.

Caesar's calendar—or the Julian Calendar—stood the test of time for the next 12 centuries.

You might recognize the names of our months in the names the Romans used for months all those hundreds of years ago: *Januarius, Februarius, Martius, Aprilis, Maius, Junius, Julius, Augustus, September, October, November, and December.*

brilliant orator, turning public speaking into an art form. Catullus (84–54 BCE) and Lucretius (95–55 BCE) were famous poets from the same era.

But it was under the reign of Augustus that Rome enjoyed a golden age of literature. Virgil (80–19 BCE) was one of the greatest poets of that era and ever after. His masterpiece, *Aeneid*, is full of romance, adventure, and patriotism (remember, part of *Aeneid* is about the founding of Rome). The historian Livy (59 BCE–17 CE) and the poet Horace (65–8 BCE) also wrote about Rome's destiny. Ovid (43 BCE–17 CE) was a

Interesting Tidbit:
Trajan's Column

The spiral frieze on Trajan's Column is about 650 feet long and contains no fewer than 155 different scenes. The column itself is 100 feet high and the frieze wraps around it. The most amazing thing about this frieze is not necessarily its artistic value, but its historical value. We can learn a great deal about the day by looking at, or "reading," the scenes in the frieze. This frieze depicts Emperor Trajan's conquest over Dacia.

supreme storyteller and his bold poems are regarded as some of the finest ever written.

In the second century CE Apuleius wrote one of the most popular works of Latin literature, *Metamorphoses*, also called *The Golden Ass*. This novel tells of the adventures of Lucius, who plays around with magic and accidentally transforms himself into a donkey.

Roman Clothing and Fashion

Much of what we know about Roman clothing comes from how people were shown in statues, paintings, and mosaics, or how they were written about in literature. Because it was usually the rich portrayed in art and literature, we don't know a lot about how common people might have dressed or worn their hair.

The most basic garment of clothing in ancient Rome was the *tunica*. The *tunica* was usually sleeveless and fell to about the knee. It was decorated with wide purple trim for senators and thin purple trim for magistrates. All other citizens wore plain white *tunicas*.

Men wore a toga over the *tunica*. This was a large white cloth made of wool that was wrapped around the body in a particular way, leaving the right arm free. Until they were initiated into manhood at age 16, boys wore the toga *praetexta,* which was decorated with a purple strip. After the ceremony, they traded in their old toga for a toga *virilis*, which was all white.

Over the *tunica*, girls and women wore a *stola*, a short-sleeved dress fastened at the waist by a belt, and carefully folded to create elegant pleats. Cloaks with hoods were worn over the *stola* when women went outside.

Women's hairstyles changed over time. Initially, hairstyles were plain—pulled back into a ponytail or into a simple bun at the neck. During the Augustan period, hairstyles began to grow fancier, and by Trajan's time in the first century CE they had become elaborate constructions of curls. Women curled their hair with a *calamistrum*, a hollow iron that was heated on a brazier (like a little grill). They also used hairpins, ribbons, wigs, and hairpieces to add volume to their hairstyles.

Wealthier matrons often had their hair and makeup done by a slave— an *ornatrix*—who specialized in beauty treatments. Hair was often dyed or bleached a reddish-blonde. Makeup was liberally applied. As a foundation, women used a layer of white lead mixed with honey and some type of oil. Sometimes the lead was mixed with dyes (such as red ocher or wine dregs) to give a pinker tint. Next, the face was sprinkled with finely ground hematite to give it a sparkly appearance. Eyelashes and eyebrows were highlighted with soot and the eyelids were given green or blue eye shadow.

Men were clean shaven until Emporer Hadrian's day in the early second century CE (100s). Hadrian wore a full beard to cover a disfigurement and, in doing so, set a new style. Care of the hair and the

Interesting Tidbit: Hair for Wigs

German women often provided hair for use in wigs and hairpieces. Their hair was preferred, probably because it was blond in color.

Out of the Mouths of Romans

Pliny the Elder gives cosmetic tips.

"Asses' milk is believed to remove wrinkles from the skin of the face and make it soft and white; certain women are known to treat their cheeks exactly seven times a day. It was Poppea, the wife of the emperor Nero, who started this fashion; she also used it to bath in, which is why she took herds of asses with her on journeys."

Interesting Tidbit:
Death Masks

Patrician families made wax death masks (created by molding wax over the faces of a dead person). Death masks were made of important people in the family and were then hung in a cabinet as a kind of visual family tree.

beard meant frequent trips to the barber shop, which, like today, served as a place where men traded ideas and gossip.

Beautiful jewelry was worn for every occasion. Rings, bracelets, necklaces, hairpins, and brooches of gold, pearls, and emeralds were common. Cameos were very popular and showed up in pendants, rings, and brooches. These carved stones were made of materials such as rock crystal, agate, or even glass paste. Scenes on cameos ranged from portraits to mythological stories. Men often wore a ring—one was preferred, but some wore many.

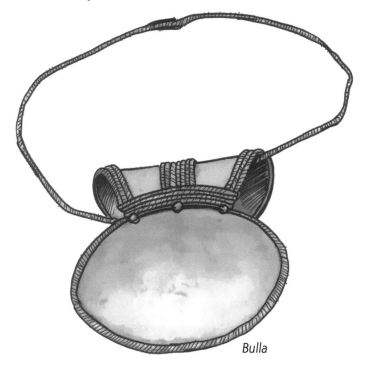

Bulla

activity: **Bulla**

This is the little pouch that all children wore around their necks.
The bulla carried items or charms that were thought to protect them from harm.

1 Fold your square of felt in half, and cut according to the diagram. Take one of the pieces, and, keeping it folded, cut the corners off the folded side to make the bottom rounded.

2 Thread your needle with the brown thread and sew the two sides. Turn the little pouch right side out (the sewed part will be on the inside now).

3 Find some little items you really like: some smooth rounded stones, little figures, or a special coin—and place them in your *bulla*.

4 Tie the *bulla* shut with a piece of string making sure you have really long ends to the string. Tie the ends together and hang your *bulla* around your neck.

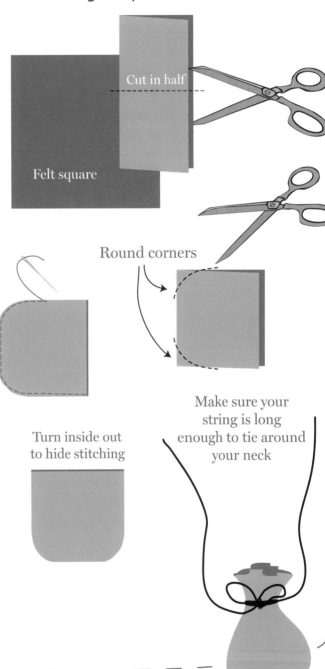

Cut in half

Felt square

Round corners

Turn inside out
to hide stitching

Make sure your
string is long
enough to tie around
your neck

supplies

a square of felt
preferably brown

scissors

needle & brown thread

little favorite items

string

Discover how
the Roman Army
conquered the
civilized world

Learn who the
soldiers were
and how they
lived on the road

See what
motivated the
soldier to march
on through
hard times

The Mighty Roman Army

ROMAN MILITARY HISTORY CAN BE DIVIDED INTO five important periods: the wars they fought with their neighbors on the Italian peninsula (509–270 BC); the Punic Wars (264–146 BCE); the Social Wars (91–88 BCE); the wars of expansion outside the Italian peninsula (58 BCE–200 CE); and the Wars of Attrition (early 200s–476 CE). After a brief discussion of the general structure and technique of the military, we'll explore how it changed from one stage to the next.

The Roman Military

Until its collapse, the Roman military featured a system of legions (hence the word legionnaire, which means "soldier"). A legion was made up of 10 cohorts, and a cohort was made up of three maniples. Each maniple was made up of two centuries, and a century was a unit of 100 soldiers. That would make each legion 6,000 soldiers strong. As far as leadership went, a centurion commanded a century, and six tribunes commanded each legion. As the empire expanded, the army grew to a point where two consuls, who were elected for one-year terms, split the army in half to make it more manageable.

When legions went into battle, soldiers were organized into a **phalanx**—a square of spearman spaced so closely together that their shields locked, making a nearly impenetrable fighting machine. Lightly armored troops would fight skirmishes (little fights) on the edges of the phalanx. The poorest soldiers usually served as skirmishers, because they couldn't afford the heavy armor, javelins, or swords used by soldiers in the phalanx. Skirmishers went into battle with little more than a small round shield, a dull sword, and a helmet covered with wolfskin. They accounted for about 1,200 men in every legion.

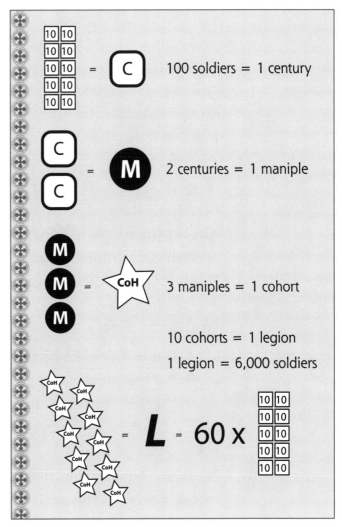

100 soldiers = 1 century

2 centuries = 1 maniple

3 maniples = 1 cohort

10 cohorts = 1 legion

1 legion = 6,000 soldiers

KNOW YOUR ANCIENT ROMAN *Army*

phalanx: a square of spearman spaced so closely together that their shields locked.

Wars with its neighbors on the Italian peninsula is considered an important period of Roman military history. During these battles, the Roman army first learned how to fight and rule conquered territories effectively with a large group of soldiers. One important lesson they learned was that if they built all-weather roads to and within the defeated territories, it was easier to protect their conquests (see chapter 5 to read more about Roman roads). Also, they figured out how to set up colonies of people loyal to Rome, and the importance of establishing military bases. They carried this knowledge with them for centuries to come.

The Punic Wars

Shortly after Rome had gained complete control of the entire Italian peninsula, the second major period of their military history began, the Punic Wars period. There were three Punic Wars, all of which were fought against the state of Carthage in Northern Africa. From the outset of these conflicts it was clear that whoever won them would control the Mediterranean Sea and all the valuable trade that took place on its waters.

The Romans never had a sea presence until the Punic Wars. They captured a Carthaginian ship and then copied it and created a fleet. They added an innovation called a *corvus* to the war ship—a bridge with

KNOW YOUR ANCIENT ROMAN *Army*

booty: money and belongings that a conquering army takes from people of conquered lands.

palisade wall: a defensive wall lined with pointed logs facing outward. See picture above.

auxiliaries: Roman troops recruited from territories conquered by the Roman army.

a spike that could be lowered from the deck of a Roman ship onto their opponent's ship. This locked the two ships together and allowed Roman soldiers to board the enemy ship and engage in hand-to-hand combat. The *corvus* made the Roman ship top-heavy, though, and in bad weather the ship tended to capsize. Back to the drawing board.

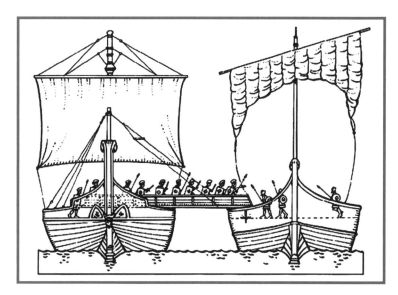

The Social Wars

The brief but important period known as the Social Wars (91–88 BCE) resulted from the Roman military having to deal with the pressures of having taken on so many provinces on the Italian peninsula. Although it had been a long while since these provinces had been acquired, in 91 BCE the men of these colonies finally worked up the courage to fight against Rome for Roman citizenship and the rights they would gain by becoming citizens. As it was, they were paying taxes to Rome and obeying Roman law with-

Spartacus and His Slave Revolt

Spartacus was a captured soldier from Thrace that was sold as a slave to work on a gladiator. Having fought against the Roman army, he knew how the Roman army fought. In 73 BCE he and 70 others escaped from slavery and hid on Mount Vesuvius. He raised an army of 90,000 men with whom he defeated two Roman legions. All told, Spartacus skirmished with the Roman army for about two years. Finally, Marcus Licinius Crassus routed Spartacus in 71 BCE and, to make an example, crucified 6,000 of Spartacus's soldiers, placing them every 30 yards along the road out of Rome.

Out of the Mouths of Romans

Crassus on the Slave Revolt

"One Lentulus Batiates trained up a great many gladiators in Capua, most of them Gauls and Thracians, who, not for any fault by them committed, but simply through the cruelty of their master, were kept in confinement for this object of fighting one with another. Two hundred of these formed a plan to escape, but being discovered, those of them who became aware of it in time to anticipate their master, being seventy-eight, got out of a cook's shop chopping-knives and spits, and made their way through the city, and lighting by the way on several wagons that were carrying gladiators' arms to another city, they seized upon them and armed themselves..."

out the privileges they deserved in return. When the Senate realized that these individuals would continue to fight until they got what they wanted, they enacted a law that was similar to the laws introduced by the Gracchus brothers before their murders in 133 and 121 BCE. They granted both land and citizenship to landless Romans and colonists on the Italian peninsula who laid down their arms within 60 days. Suddenly, the Roman army had a much larger pool of citizens to draw from.

With ever-growing numbers of landless troops joining the military, military leaders gained power, for it was they—not the Senate—who paid their troops the land they earned for their military service. Julius Caesar was probably the most gifted of these leaders. More than the other army commanders, he was able to win over and keep hold of his troops' loyalty. He could lead his troops anywhere. Why? Because he followed through with the promises he made, he inspired them with his words, and he made all of his men—even the low-ranked skirmishers—feel important. Furthermore, unlike most commanders, whenever Caesar conquered a city, he did not take more than his share of the booty. He left much of it for his men and made sure it was fairly divided.

Q: What was at the root of the *Social Wars?*

The Wars of Expansion

Caesar valued military glory as much as anything. So when he became dictator in 46 BCE, the fourth major period in Roman military history—the wars of expansion—began. Under Caesar, Rome defeated the Celtic Gauls and Britain. The Roman military, which was already the biggest and fastest moving military in the world, grew even larger and faster.

Throughout the wars of expansion, the Roman army traveled with incredible speed and efficiency. Not only did they march fast (often thanks to their own excellent roads), but they set up camp fast, too. At the end of a hard day's march of 15 miles, the soldiers set up a virtual fortress in a very short time. They surrounded the perimeter of the camp with a ditch and a wall of pointed wooden logs called a palisade wall that faced out to prevent enemies from getting inside. Just think about all the work that took—clearing space, digging the ditch, and felling trees for the palisade wall. And this was all after a long day's march.

As the Roman Empire pushed farther and farther into the known world the armies got farther from the center of power—Rome—and relied more heavily on non-citizen soldiers, and auxiliaries. It became increasingly difficult to maintain the peace both within the army and in the territories.

Interesting Tidbit: Auxiliary troops

Even with land and citizenship reforms made as a result of the Social Wars, there weren't enough Roman men to serve. More and more, Rome recruited men from newly conquered territories. These men were called "auxiliary" troops and they served in units of 500 to 1,000 men. Auxiliary troops and their descendents were rewarded with Roman citizenship after 25 years of service.

By the time Hadrian came along as emperor (117–138 CE), the wars of expansion sparked by Caesar were nearing their end. Hadrian put more energy into maintaining the widespread borders. In Britain, Hadrian built an 80-mile-long

Hadrian's Wall.

fortified stone wall that separated England from Scotland. The idea was to protect Roman interests to the south and to prevent the Picts and other Scots to the north from invading. Hadrian's Wall included elaborate pit traps dug in front of the wall and towers placed at strategic points to better observe enemy movements.

The Wars of Attrition

By the time the Roman military entered into the fifth and final major period of its thousand-year history, the Wars of Attrition (or the how-to-lose-the-empire-bit-by-bit phase), feelings about the Roman army had changed. It was no longer seen as a privilege and duty to serve in the army. Rather, the army was having a hard time filling its ranks and men were deserting. Increasingly the Roman army had to rely on recruiting men from the outlying provinces. These recruits never felt the same kind of allegiance to Rome as those who lived closer to the seat of power.

Under Diocletian, emperor from 284 to 305 CE, the separation of the army and the state was formalized. He divided the army into the **field army** and the frontier troops. The field army went on **campaigns** into new territories. The frontier army stayed behind in the strongholds to make sure they didn't lose any territory.

This division would be the beginning of the end of the mighty Roman Empire. Dividing the once great army would eventually pit Roman soldiers against each other out on the battlefield. As the succession of emperors slipped into chaos, so did the army, making it unable to unite against invaders.

KNOW YOUR ANCIENT ROMAN *Army*

field army: the core of troops that went out on campaigns.

campaign: any military effort to conquer new territory or defeat enemies.

frontier army: the troops who defended Roman borders and strongholds.

CHAPTER

Learn about
the Coliseum's
original purpose,
builder, and
design

Find out about
one of history's
deadliest volcanic
eruptions

See the
beginning of
the empire's
decline

The Next Two Hundred Years

IN A SINGLE YEAR AFTER NERO'S DEATH IN 68 CE, FOUR different men tried to reign as emperor, and they were all disasters. The last of the four, Vitellius, was particularly bad. He squandered his money on unnecessary luxuries. For one banquet, he reportedly served 2,000 fish and 7,000 birds to his guests. He spent 900 million *sestertii* on dining alone (the yearly salary for a million Roman soldiers!). Eventually, Titus Flavius Vespasian, a military general who had been stationed in Egypt, fought his way into Rome and took charge.

Vespasian

Vespasian was emperor for 10 years, from 69 to 79 CE. He was the first Roman equite (member of the middle class) to reach the pinnacle of power. Having served with the military all over the empire, he proved to be a very able ruler. He was down to earth, understood the financial aspects of running an empire, and embarked on a number of public building projects. The most famous building from his era was called Flavian's Amphitheater when it was built, but we call it the Coliseum.

Vespasian also strengthened the governments of the provinces, or provincial governments, around the empire. He extended Roman citizenship to people who lived in the provinces, which eventually allowed some of them to sit in the Senate. He beefed up Rome's border defenses, and he moved regional military recruits from their home territories to other parts of the empire. Why? Because Vespasian was interested in spreading Rome's influence to the far reaches of the empire. He knew that if military recruits stayed close to home, they wouldn't have any incentive to think like Romans. But if they were in foreign territory, they would have to rely more on their superiors and fellow soldiers and would thus become more "Roman."

Titus

Titus (emperor from 79 to 81 CE) succeeded his father Vespasian. He proved to be a kind, intelligent, and compassionate ruler. In his first year, the volcano Mount Vesuvius blew its top and rained up to 20 feet of ash on the cities of Pompeii and Herculaneum. Thousands of people died and Titus helped with disaster relief. We can think of him as the emperor of disaster because soon after Vesuvius erupted, there was a major fire in Rome, and right after that a plague swept through Italy. Titus met each challenge head-on and with generosity. The public loved him. On his deathbed he said, "I have made only one mistake." He died before he could explain this mistake. To this day, no one knows what he meant.

The Coliseum got its name because it was near the spot where a colossal statue of Nero once stood.

Interesting Tidbit:
The Coliseum

The Coliseum (or Flavian's Amphitheater)

The Coliseum was a remarkable structure, one of the finest architectural achievements in the history of the Roman empire. This building, which looks like a series of arches placed one on top of the other, was created by Emperor Vespasian to remind the Roman people that they lived in the greatest, most powerful nation in the world. The stadium was oval in shape, seated about 55,000 people, and was the site of entertainment on a grand scale, including the bloody gladiator games. There was, a common saying that goes: "When the Coliseum falls, so falls Rome and all the world."

Domitian

Titus left no heir but his brother, Domitian (emperor 81–96 CE) moved in to fill the void. By all accounts he was a very able administrator. He completed public works and building projects begun by his father and brother, and he put down rebellions in some of the outlying provinces. He also raised the pay of men serving in the army.

But Domitian was hated. Why? Because he acted like a dictator. Okay, he *was* a dictator—like the emperors before him, he had all the power—but the Romans didn't appreciate him acting that way. He built an enormous imperial palace and walked around in royal garb. He disregarded the Senate. He wanted to be known as *dominus et deus*—lord and god—and saw himself as the center of Roman religion. Failure to worship the emperor and imperial gods became an act of treason under his reign.

names *you should know*

Pliny the Elder [Gaius Plinius Secundus] (23–79 CE)

A Roman lawyer, Pliny the Elder wrote a 32-book encyclopedia titled *Natural History*. When Mount Vesuvius erupted in 79 CE, he went to Pompeii by boat to help rescue survivors who were on the beach. He died there, probably overtaken by the poisonous gas.

Eventually, Domitian became paranoid and saw conspiracies everywhere he looked. Finally, his wife, the Praetorian Guard, imperial servants, and high-ranking senators conspired to have him murdered. Rome celebrated.

Trajan

Nerva (emperor from 96 to 98 CE) was appointed emperor by the Senate when Domitian was killed. Nerva knew he wasn't up to the task and, in a shrewd move, adopted Marcus Ulpius Trajanus (Trajan) as his heir in 97 CE.

Q: *Why is Pompeii so well preserved?*

Trajan, who ruled the empire for almost 20 years (98–117 CE), proved to be one of Rome's most popular emperors. He fought wars in Dacia

names *you should know*

Trajan [Marcus Ulpius Trajanus] (c. 53–117 CE)

Trajan, from southern Spain, was the first emperor to be born outside of Rome (although he was raised in Rome). As emperor, he was known as a generous and fair leader. He built many buildings throughout the empire and created the public baths in Rome itself. Under his rule, the empire annexed the territory north of the Danube River in a victory commemorated on Trajan's Column.

Plutarch (50–120 CE)

A Greek writer and a Roman citizen, Plutarch wrote *The Parallel Lives*, which looked at the careers of great men in the history of Greece and Rome. A lot of what we know about early Romans and Greeks comes from Plutarch.

Pompeii and Herculaneum

In 79 CE, the volcano Vesuvius erupted and rained volcanic ash and pumice down on the city of Pompeii. The ash didn't kill the 3,600 people who died in Pompeii—it was the volcanic gas.

In Herculaneum, a mud flow and debris collapsed buildings and trapped people beneath them. The mud flow hit with the force of an atomic bomb and carried much of the town several miles away.

Today, these two cities are remarkably well preserved, particularly Pompeii, which lay buried under up to 20 feet of ash for almost two millennia. We've learned much about the architecture, art, and daily life of the first-century CE Roman Empire from archeological excavations of these cities.

The buried town of Pompeii was discovered in 1748 and archeological excavations began in 1860. Much of Pompeii has been restored and has been visited by millions of people. Beautiful villas—complete with frescoes and mosaics—were perfectly preserved by the ash, along with shops and inns along the main road. There were also some gruesome finds, such as "casts" made in the ash of people and animals as they were asphyxiated by the poison gas (they're casts because the actual bodies have disintegrated). Pompeii offers a vivid picture of what life was like in this thriving port city when it was encapsulated in ash in 79 CE.

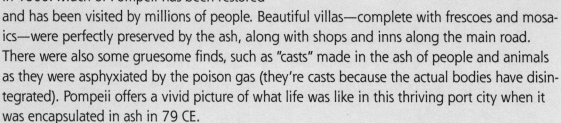

Out of the Mouths of Romans

Graffiti found in Pompeii

"Celadus, the Thracian, makes all the girls sigh."

"Crescens, the net fighter, holds the hearts of all the girls."

(Romania), Armenia, and Mesopotamia. His exploits in Dacia were documented on an exquisite 100-foot column engraved with a spiraling bas relief known as Trajan's Column. He built fabulous public buildings in Rome including the magnificent Roman Forum, the market, a basilica, public baths, and libraries.

Trajan also realized that the health of the empire depended on the health of its citizens. Trajan believed the government should pay for education and food for needy families and children throughout Italy. This system was called *alimenta*.

Trajan died while on a military campaign to the east where he was trying to expand the empire, yet again. After his death, every new emperor was honored by the Senate with the prayer *felicior Augusto, melior Traiano* (may he be luckier than Augustus and better than Trajan). His honorable reputation has remained intact for 1,900 years.

Hadrian

Publius Aelius Hadrianus (Hadrian) succeeded Trajan in 117 CE and ruled the empire for the next 21 years. With Trajan having been so popular, Hadrian had big shoes to fill. What made this an even harder task was that Trajan left behind a Rome that was stretched thin. He'd poured money into defending an empire that was crumbling around the edges. Hadrian believed that a return to a non-expansionist Rome—a Rome with clearly defined borders—would make for a stronger empire. He gave up some of the recently conquered land in the east and strengthened some of the other borders, including building Hadrian's Wall to defend the northern border of the empire in Britain.

Out of the Mouths of Romans

Pliny the Younger

Nephew of Pliny the Elder, Pliny the Younger wrote about the eruption of Mount Vesuvius in what remains as the only recorded eyewitness account of the incident.

"You could hear the groans of the women, the cries of the children and the clamor of the men; some loudly sought their parents, others their children, others again their spouses, and recognized them by their voices.; there were some who, for fear of death, invoked it; many raised their arms to the gods, but still more said there were no more gods, and that this was the last night of the world . . ."

Hadrian was not well-liked in Rome, and he spent a good deal of his time traveling throughout the empire. He reformed the military—where he was adored as a commander—by bringing more discipline to the army. He also extended the system of *alimenta*.

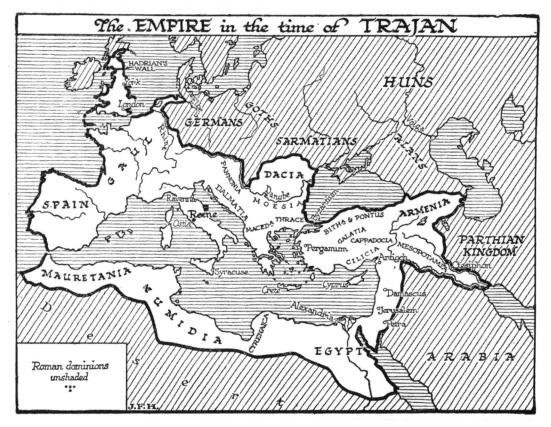

The EMPIRE in the time of TRAJAN

Roman dominions unshaded

There are some spectacular buildings created by Hadrian that are still standing, including his mausoleum (known today as Castel San Angelo) and his villa in Tivoli. He adopted Antoninus Pius as his successor.

Antoninus Pius and Marcus Aurelius

Antoninus Pius, who was emperor from 138 to 161 CE, was not a remarkable ruler. Although he had a lengthy reign, not much has been written about him. He never left Italy, and his most significant reforms were in

names *you should know*

Hadrian [Publius Aelius Hadrianus] (ruled 117–138 CE)

Hadrian was proclaimed emperor the day after his adoptive father, Trajan, died. Hadrian's rule is marked by extensive building projects throughout the empire, one of the most famous being Hadrian's Wall in Britain.

Hadrian coin.

the courts. Two legal principles Antoninus developed that you might be familiar with are the notion of presuming someone innocent until proven guilty, and the idea that in the case of a tie verdict, the person accused of the crime is given the benefit of the doubt. Antoninus didn't pay much attention to military affairs, and by the time of his death, there was plenty of trouble on the borders of Rome.

"felicior Augusto, melior Traiano"
may he be luckier than Augustus and better than Trajan

Marcus Aurelius

Marcus Aurelius, who was the nephew of Hadrian, was adopted by Antoninus so he could be the successor. When he was appointed emperor in 161 CE, Marcus insisted that his close friend, Lucius Varus, act as co-emperor. They worked together until Varus's death in 169 CE.

Marcus was relentless in his quest to hold the empire together. He defended Rome's borders, issued imperial decisions, and heard legal cases. While trying to hold back invasions along the Danube River, he wrote *Meditations*, a simple reflective journal.

Chaos and Many Emperors

When Marcus died in 180 CE, the empire was slipping into a period of decline and fragmentation. For the next 100 years, until the reign of Diocletian in 285 CE, Rome was ruled by a series of emperors who went from bad to worse and back again. Most of the rulers and their families during this period ended up being killed in very gruesome ways.

Q: What judicial reforms did *Antoninus Pius* make?

Also during this 100-year period where one bad leader was assasinated only to be followed by the next, military legions began to promote their

Interesting Tidbit:
What's in a name?

Look at the names of the tribes of people who were invading Rome because you might recognize them. We still use the word *vandal* to describe someone who destroys something. "Goth" is at the root of the word *Gothic*. "Franks" come from a place that we now call France.

commanders to serve as emperors. There were at least 25 of these "barracks emperors" who ruled during this century, with 16 of them ruling between the years 244 and 260. It's hard to imagine anyone wanting to be emperor during this time because it seemed like an immediate death sentence. To make matters worse, the Roman Empire was being attacked from all sides. The Franks, Jutes, and Germanic Alemanni invaded across the Rhine River, and the Vandals and Goths crossed the Danube River. If this weren't enough, the Persian Empire had begun to creep westward toward the Roman Empire.

In the meantime, provinces began to split off from the empire and fend for themselves. Parts of France, Germany, Britain, and Spain formed the Gallic Empire in 260 CE with a capital in Trier (Germany), ruled by Emperor Tetricus. The areas now inhabited by the countries Syria, Palestine, and Egypt, as well as large parts of Asia Minor also formed their own empire. It was called the Palmyrene Empire, named after the ancient city of Palmyra, and it was ruled by Queen Zenobia.

A series of emperors gradually conquered the Goths, stabilized the center of the empire, and reunited the eastern and western portions that had broken away. One of the most important of these emporers was Aurelian. He brought the Palmyrene Empire in the east back under Roman control in 274 CE and, in the same year, defeated the Gallic Empire in the west. He is best remembered for constructing a massive defensive wall around Rome that still bears his name.

names *you should know*

Commodus (ruled from 180 to 192 CE)

Commodus was chosen emperor upon the death of his father, Marcus Aurelius. He was 18 at the time and put the running of the government in the hands of advisors while he acted like a teenager, racing chariots and playing at being a gladiator. The senators were disgusted. Soon Commodus wanted to be known as Hercules and wore a Hercules outfit while participating in sporting events. He then wanted Rome to be renamed *Colonia Commodianna*, or, "Colony of Commodus." Commodus was killed by a group of senators and his favorite girlfriend.

Aurelian met an untimely death at the hands of his own men in 275 CE. For the next decade, the empire was ruled by six emperors who were all put in place by legions (barracks emperors) and then murdered by those who put them in power. Rome was not a safe place to be if you were an emperor.

Q:Describe the Aurelian Wall.

Within the 200 years covered in this chapter, the government of the Roman empire went from caring and stable to disjointed and chaotic. But life goes on, and even during this time of government disintegration, people turned to entertainment to pass the time.

The Aurelian Wall

In 271 CE Aurelian recognized the vulnerability of Rome and constructed a massive defensive wall around the city. It's about 12 miles long and originally contained 18 gates. Today you can find its remains all around the city of Rome, which has grown far beyond the borders defined by the Aurelian Wall.

activity: **Laurel Wreath**

Emperors wore wreaths made from laurel (bay leaves) on special occasions.

1 Take a couple of pipe cleaners and connect them to make a circle that will fit around your head.

2 Fold your green paper in half and cut out the shape of a laurel leaf. See diagram.

4 Place on your head and feel like an emperor.

You might want to try different kinds of paper—tissue paper, construction paper, or shiny green wrapping paper—to see which leaves you like the most.

3 Open up the leaf so you have two leaves connected by a stem. Fold each of these leaves around the pipe cleaner, using a drop of glue to keep the leaves in place. Place the leaves pointing in different directions so that they all aren't sticking up or sticking down.

supplies

pipe cleaners

green paper

glue

Learn about the Roman sport of chariot racing

Meet the gladiators behind the masks

Compare Roman athletes to the star athletes of today

That's Entertainment

THE EARLIEST GAMES AND FESTIVALS, or *ludi*, in ancient Rome were religious celebrations. A *ludi* could last several days and there might be up to a dozen *ludi* throughout the calendar year. Stages were erected for dramatic performances associated with the festival and then taken down. This went on for hundreds of years until Pompey built and dedicated the first permanent theater building in 55 BCE.

Theater was popular but ancient Romans were just wild for chariot racing and staged gladiator battles that took place in the Coliseum.

Chariot Racing

Chariot racing was one of the most popular sports in both the Greek and Roman worlds. Originally, wealthy Greek aristocrats from all over the Hellenistic (Greek) world competed against each other in the "sport of kings." While the Greeks enjoyed chariot racing they did not take it as seriously as the Romans, whose entire culture became obsessed by it.

Out of the Mouths of Romans

Juvenal

A second-century CE satirist, Juvenal wrote that the two things yearned for by the Roman mob were bread and circuses (panem a circenses).

Early on in Rome, chariot racing became a professional sport. There were four teams that competed against each other—Red, White, Blue, and Green—and a day at the races involved heavy betting on your favorite team. The chariot racing industry was set up much like NASCAR is today. There were professional drivers, fantastic horses bred for racing, and sleek chariots all competing against each other for a purse. When an official decided to put on a chariot race, he paid each team a certain amount of money for participating and then

the winner received the prize money. Purses for the big races were often between 40,000 and 60,000 *sestertii* (remember that a Roman soldier earned only 900 *sestertii* a year!).

Circus Maximus

The place where chariot races occurred was called the circus. In the early years, chariot races took place on an oval track surrounded by bleacher-style seating. Emperor Trajan built the Circus Maximus. The new circus was 600 meters long and could accommodate up to 180,000 spectators, making it the largest single complex for public congregation in the world (compare this with the New Orleans Superdome, which holds 72,000 spectators).

The track was divided with a barrier down the middle, which kept chariots from cutting corners as they raced. On top of the barrier were a number of sculptures that served as lap-counting devices. There were two lap-counting mechanisms: the seven gilded eggs and the seven gilded dolphins. As the lead chariots rounded the corners, the lap counters would be flipped (you knew what end of the track you were at if you saw either an egg or a dolphin). At either end was a turning point in the form of a large gilded cone.

Races lasted for seven laps, which worked out to about five and a quarter miles. The two, four, or sometimes even six-horse chariots lined up at the starting gate with grooms to hold them in position. (Emperor Nero even tried to race a ten-horse team.) At the horn, the horses leaped forward and the race was on!

"panem e circenses"
bread and circuses

Chariots were small vehicles with wheels about the size of wheelchair wheels and a platform just big enough to hold a standing driver. Keeping this thing upright while making tight turns took a very skillful driver. Even so, there were many crashes, much to the thrill of the spectators. Chariot racing was a no-holds-barred event and drivers would do just about anything they could to win. There were no rules saying you couldn't whip another driver's horse or ram into the side of his chariot. The fans could be rowdy, often provoking fights before, during, and after the races. It was a wild place to be, and clearly a lot of people loved it.

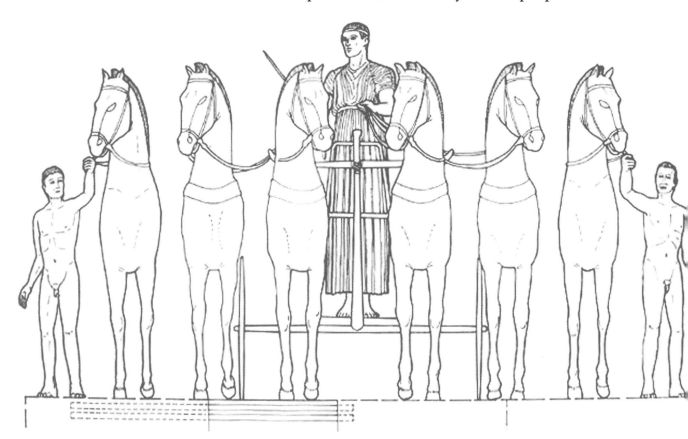

Who were the drivers? They often began life as slaves or were the children of drivers. Winning drivers became celebrities (and, like today's celebrities, were hounded any time they went out in public). Some went on to buy their freedom—if they lived long enough. Scorpus, a late-first-century charioteer won an amazing 2,048 victories before dying in a crash around the age of 27.

Gladiatorial Combat

Gladiatorial combat began in Etruria as part of aristocratic funeral games and sacrifices. When the gladiator games were introduced to Rome in the third century BCE, the Roman aristocracy was very keen to adopt the practice. They hosted lavish games that included gladiator combat as a way to increase their own popularity with the common people as well as with influential Romans. By the first century BCE, gladiatorial combat was a lucrative sport for the *lanistae* (owners/ managers) of gladiatorial troops who traveled in the wake of the Roman army, offering to put on matches for a handsome fee.

Gladiatorial contests were originally held in places like the marketplace or the forum with only a few pairs of gladiators fighting at a time. As the popularity of these contests soared, it became necessary to build a permanent structure for the games. In 80 CE the Coliseum was completed for this purpose. Under the Coliseum's wood-floored arena were cells and small rooms where the criminals, animals, and gladiators were kept before the games. For the inauguration of the Coliseum there were 100 consecutive days of games.

Who were the gladiators? Just like many charioteers, they were slaves, men captured in war, or criminals. Every now and then a desperate citizen signed up for gladiator school in hopes of making some money.

KNOW YOUR ANCIENT ROMAN *Gladiators*

There were different types of gladiators. Some specialized in strength and armor, while others relied on speed and mobility. The two types were often pitted against each other in the arena.

The heavily armed fighters:

Secutores carried a huge rectangular shield; a sword; a heavy, simple helmet with eyeholes; one protective arm sleeve, and a protective *greave* (shin guard) for their forward leg.

Thraeces had a helmet with a wide brim, crest, and protective visor. They were armed with a curved sword called a *scimitar*—and a small shield, and wore *greaves* on both legs.

Myrmillones were heavily armed fighters who were named for the emblem of a fish on their helmets. Their curved sword, which got wider toward the pointed end, was called a *scimitar*.

The lightly armed fighters:

Retiarii were armed with nets and tridents.

Laquearii were armed with a lasso.

Sagittarii were armed with a bow and arrows.

Essedarii fought one another from chariots.

Dimachaeri fought with two swords.

Andabatae were riders in armor who fought with closed visors, which, in effect, made them blind.

Sometimes, men were sold to a gladiator school where they came under the supervision of a trainer and an owner. They had to swear an oath of complete submission and agree "to be burned, to be bound, to be beaten, and to be killed by the sword." They trained with heavier weapons than they would use in the games to build up their muscles, and competed three or four times a year. Most gladiators died in the

arena—killed by wild animals like lions and tigers or by members of their own gladiator school. Those who survived could hope to win their freedom and the "wooden sword" that was given to retired gladiators.

Good gladiators, like good chariot drivers, became wildly popular with the public.

Executions usually served as the warm-up to the contests between gladiators. Often criminals sentenced to execution were pitted against each other. One would be armed and the other unarmed, and the winner would then face the next criminal, until they were all dead.

A day at the games might begin with wild animals being pitted against one another (the Romans were responsible for killing thousands of wild and exotic animals that were imported to Rome from the far reaches of the empire). Then the execution of the criminals would follow.

The afternoon featured gladiator pairs. Each fight was refereed, and if the referee thought they weren't fighting hard enough, he would literally whip them along. When a gladiator was wounded or defeated, he could ask for mercy and concede defeat by holding up his index finger. It was up to the sponsor of the games as to whether he lived or died—a thumbs up meant the gladiator should live to fight another day, and a thumbs down meant he should die. The crowd really got into it by cheering and waving and making their wishes known.

Porta Libitinensis, or Death's Gate.

If the gladiator was to die, he was supposed to die bravely and with honor. After the death blow was delivered, he was dragged off by a slave out of the arena through the Porta Libitinensis, or Death's Gate.

In a spectacle even greater than the gladiator games, sea battles were enacted on artificial lakes created by flooding arenas. Emperor Augustus even created an artificial lake next to the Tiber River—it was drainable so it wouldn't smell between battles. Thousands of men took part in these battles and the survivors, if they had fought well, could go free.

Why did the Romans like these gruesome games involving life and death? No one can really answer that. Perhaps it was a way for people to keep their minds off of the larger problems around them—like the failing health of their empire. Whatever the case, it's impossible for you or me to fathom killing and mutilating people for sport—and it's comforting to know that many writers of the day deplored the violent nature of the games.

Out of the Mouths of Romans

Pylades to Augustus

"It is to your advantage, Caesar, that we keep the public occupied."

Pylades was referring to the Roman games.

The Rise of the Empire, Again

WHEN WE LAST LOOKED AT THE EMPIRE IN ABOUT 284 CE, it was a mess. Although Aurelian tried to knit the empire back together when he brought the Gallic and the Palmyrene Empires back under Roman control, the empire was still like a loosely stitched scarf that could unravel at any moment.

The Tetrarchy

Diocletian, who was emperor from 284 to 305 CE, and who split the army in two, faced a horrendous challenge. How was he going to reestablish firm central authority? First of all, he felt that succession needed to be predictable to lessen competition for the position of emperor. And, secondly, he realized that he needed the help of someone he trusted to help him rule. The empire was too big to rule alone.

He brought in a right hand man, Maximian, and gave him the title *Caesar* (junior emperor), as well as the western side of the empire to rule. Diocletian himself would remain *Augustus* (senior emperor), with power to govern the east.

Even with this new arrangement, both rulers had their hands full with half of the empire. So Diocletian appointed two more caesars as helpers. Both of his choices had impressive military backgrounds and were required to marry into the two emperors' families. Constantius married Maximian's daughter and helped rule the west, and Galerius married Diocletian's daughter and helped rule the east. The empire was now ruled by a tetrarchy, or four rulers.

Diocletian

Constantine

While the tetrarchy arranged by Diocletian worked for a time, it began to fail when Constantius (who had risen to *Augustus* after Diocletian and Maximian's retirement) died. At the time of Constantius's death, his son and junior emperor, Constantine, took over his domain. Constantine had a powerful personality and didn't want help ruling in the west. By 312 CE, five years after his father's death, he defeated Maxentius, Maximian's son, to become sole ruler of the west. In 324 CE, the tension between Constantine and his brother-in-law, Licinius, who was senior emperor of the east, boiled over into war. Constantine defeated Licinius and became sole emperor of the Roman world.

Q: *How* did workers pay their taxes under Constantine?

names *you should know*

Diocletian (emperor from 284 to 305 CE)

Diocletian rose through the military ranks to become emperor. He was responsible for bringing the empire back together and reorganizing the government. With a series of broad tax reforms he saved the central government, but it forced the common people into a system that tied them to their land and to one profession for their entire lives.

activity: **Cameo Pin**

Cameos are small scenes or figures that are carved in relief, meaning the image is raised higher than its background. Cameos are carved from one material—often coral—and are made into all different kinds of jewelry, such as necklaces, rings, and brooches. Usually the figure on a cameo is a profile of someone. It's likely that the rulers in the tetrarchy and their wives would have had their images carved on cameo pins.

1 Soften a piece of clay by kneading it with your fingers. Roll it into a ball, then flatten it to create your base. Soften a smaller piece of clay, then roll it into a ball and squish it onto the base.

2 Use your knife or wooden tools to shape the clay into a profile. Make sure to make all the features—nose, eye, mouth, chin, ear, hair.

3 When you're satisfied with the way it looks, you can soften another piece of clay, then roll it into a narrow, long "snake." Place this around the edge of the base to create a decorative border.

4 Follow the directions on the package of clay and bake the pin on a cookie sheet in the oven. After your creation has baked and cooled, glue on a pin back.

supplies

Fimo or Sculpy clay
just one color

plastic knife or wooden clay tools

metal pin back
(these can be found in packages in craft stores)

glue

names *you should know*

Constantine the Great (emperor 310–337 CE)

Constantine continued the reforms begun under Diocletian, but his most significant impact on the empire had to do with his a religious conversion to Christianity in 312. Under Constantine, the Roman Catholic Church was established. He created a new capital for the Roman empire in the Greek city of Byzantium, which he rebuilt and renamed Constantinople. The Roman empire—at least the eastern Roman empire—became a Christian state.

The first thing Constantine (often called Constantine the Great) did in his new, all-powerful position was move the capital of the empire to Constantinople (ancient Byzantium, now modern Istanbul). Why did he do this? Because he thought he needed a break with the past, which was represented by the now-isolated city of Rome. Constantine chose four prefects to rule over four other areas of the empire, but he maintained complete control over the military.

Constantine continued an economic program started by Diocletian. When workers paid their taxes, they paid "in kind," which meant if you made olive oil, you paid in olive oil. Workers were organized into guilds—like unions—and weren't allowed to change jobs. Sons were required to do the same kind of job their fathers did. This allowed Constantine to figure out how much money and what kinds of goods were going to be collected by the government, but it made the people very unhappy.

In 312 CE, Constantine had a vision of a giant cross just before the decisive battle he won against Maxentius. The vision prompted him

Q: *Where* did Constantine move the capital of the Roman Empire? *What* did he name it?

to convert to Christianity. Although his conversion was not immediate, he eventually proclaimed himself the earthly representative of God and made Christianity the state religion. He called himself *Isoapostelis* (Equal of the Apostles). In 325 CE, he brought bishops from all over Europe to a Council at Nicea. There, they wrote the Nicene Creed, which lays out the basics of the Christian faith regarding the nature of God, the Trinity, and the Church. The council also established the date for Easter and organized the Catholic Church.

Although Constantine the Great went on a tremendous building campaign in Constantinople (including building an imperial palace, a Senate house, libraries, universities, a forum, fantastic churches, and a hippodrome) he did not neglect building in the former capital of Rome. He completed the Basilica of Maxentius and the last great imperial public bath. He also built the churches of St. John Lateran and St. Peter's.

Constantine died in 337 CE on his way to conquer the Persian Empire and convert it to Christianity. Under the direction of Constantine the Great, the seat of power shifted east and the empire was converted from a pagan state with many gods to a theocracy. In a theocracy, the state is ruled by one god or by someone like Constantine the Great, who felt chosen by God to rule in his name.

Learn about the pre-Christian Roman Gods

Study the link between the gods and government

See how Christianity survived and spread

Gods and Goddesses

THE ANCIENT ROMAN WORLD WAS FULL OF GODS and goddesses. Why? Because the Roman world included people from every culture of the known world, and most of these cultures had unique religious beliefs and gods.

Early Gods

The oldest religious practices centered on the home and the land. Early Romans believed that gods and spirits of the ancestors protected the family and the land. Every morning and evening the entire family gathered—including the slaves—and the paterfamilias led prayers on behalf of the family. Families prayed to the guardian spirits called Lares and Penates and to the gods Janus and Vesta. Lares protected the land and the Roman peasant as he worked the land. Janus, a two-faced god, represented and protected the entrance to the home, reassuring peasants that the house was safe while they worked the fields during the day. The Penates blessed and guarded the food and were thanked for providing food for the table. Finally, the goddess Vesta protected the hearth—the center of the home—which provided warmth, heat, and light for the family.

Early in Rome's history, a Roman state religion was established. Since the time of the kings, Romans had *pontifices* and *augurs* (priests and priest-like figures), and *collegia* (boards of priests) to oversee, perform, and organize Rome's religious rites. Romans believed that the gods would give them good harvests and victory in battle if they worshipped them properly. While today we often view religion as a personal choice, the Romans felt that praying to the gods and goddesses was the same as believing in Rome. Priests wielded a great deal of influence and the priesthood was often seen as a good stepping-stone to a political career.

Religion

As Rome became more of a regional power and a republic, it also developed into a religious center. Greek, Latin, and Etruscan gods and goddesses were folded into the existing belief system. The highest Roman god was Jove, or Jupiter. He became the divine paterfamilias, or father of the Roman people, serving

Q: *Name* some of the *guardian spirits* of the home and farm.

Augury

Augury was the art of interpreting from signs or omens, whether Jupiter, Rome's main god, would be happy or mad about a future event (like a battle). Augurs interpreted omens from observations of birds, called auspices.

Romans took the auspices before every important function, ranging from elections to battles. They watched the flight of birds or observed the feeding patterns of sacred chickens. Augurs would accompany armies and right before a battle would feed the sacred chickens. If the chickens ate a lot, it meant that Mars, the god of war, was pleased and the battle would go well. If they didn't eat much, it meant the troops should fight another day. Oftentimes, augurs, whose lives could depend on the outcome of the auspices, wouldn't feed the chickens for a while, just to make sure they ate well before the battle.

The second king of Rome appointed three augurs to look out for things in the city. By Julius Caesar's day, there were 16 official augers.

activity: **Fresco**

Frescoes often showed natural landscapes or important Roman gods and goddesses, and were found throughout the Roman Empire. Frescoes were created by painting directly on plaster that was not quite dry so that the paint soaked in. Pompeii has some gorgeous examples of fresco and mosaic work.

1 Mix up the plaster and pour it into your aluminum tin. Let it sit for at least 45 minutes. The plaster will be hard but still wet.

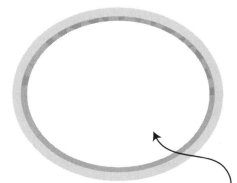

Pour plaster into aluminum tin

Start to draw design onto plaster

2 While you wait, think about what you'd like to paint. You could make some sketches to help you plan your picture.

3 Paint your picture directly on the plaster.

supplies

4 When the plaster is completely dry, remove your fresco from the aluminum tin. It should lift right out.

Finish drawing design, and start to paint it in

Plaster of Paris

aluminum tin
(any shape)

poster paints

paintbrushes

Vestal Virgins

At the center of the Forum in Rome was the Temple of Vesta, which contained a symbolic hearth tended by priestesses known as Vestal Virgins. It was a great honor to tend the hearth, and it was the duty of the priestesses to ensure the hearth's flame never went out. Romans believed that bad things would happen to Rome if the flame went out. Girls between the ages of six and ten were chosen by lottery to be Vestal Virgins. During the 30 years they spent tending the hearth, these girls and women could not marry or have relationships with men. If it was discovered that a Vestal Virgin had been with a man, she would be buried alive.

Unlike some holy women, Vestal Virgins were permitted to participate in public life. They were given the authority to pardon any criminal who walked in their path on his or her way to prison or execution, but they had to swear the accused criminal met them by accident.

as the bringer of victory, the guarantor of justice, and the highest authority. He was the god who could throw thunderbolts down from the sky. Juno, Jove's wife and the protector of women, became the materfamilias of the Roman people. Mars was the next most important god. He was the Roman god of war and defender of the city.

The following is a list of Roman gods and goddesses important during the republic. There were other gods as well, but these were the gods with Greek counterparts. As we've seen, many Romans, particularly the leaders, idealized all things Greek so it is not surprising that they borrowed and "Romanized" Greek gods.

There were other gods and goddesses as well. Saturn was the ancient god of agriculture, Ceres was the fertility goddess, Neptune was the god of all waters and seas, and Fortuna was the mistress of good luck.

Roman	Greek	Their Realm or Role
Jupiter/Jove	Zeus	rule, power, justice
Juno	Hera	protector of women
Mars	Ares	war
Minerva	Athena	wisdom, strategy, skill
Diana	Artemis	goddess of the wild
Apollo	Apollo	divine wisdom, knowledge
Vulcan	Hephaistus	fire, metallurgy
Vesta	Hestia	hearth and home
Venus	Aphrodite	love and attraction
Cupid	Eros	desire
Dis	Hades	the dead
Mercury	Hermes	boundaries, commerce
Hercules	Herakles	hero and son of Zeus

The Romans believed deeply in the power of their gods and took religion very seriously. If a Roman general won a battle, he didn't take credit for the victory. He believed it was the god acting through him who had won the battle. If the general lost the battle, it was because the gods of the other side were stronger than his god, or because he hadn't prayed or sacrificed enough to his god. The Romans believed that the more they showed their dedication to a god, the more they were given in return.

With Augustus's rise to power and the beginning of the empire, he put more emphasis on religious life. He ordered the restoration of temples that had fallen into disrepair and the revival of religious rites and festivals. Augustus thought that if people concentrated on religious activities they wouldn't pay as much attention to what was wrong with the government. For that reason he didn't care what religion people followed.

Mystery Religions

This toleration allowed new religions, called mystery religions, to spread through Rome. Mystery religions offered cleansing, purification, and salvation, as well as wild ceremonies that people enjoyed. Why are they called mystery religions? Because we don't know much about them. They all have common elements, though, including a benevolent divine figure with whom believers could have direct personal contact, secret rites, and initiation of believers into the special knowledge and understanding of the religion. The cults of Isis, Mithras, and Cybele were a few of the most prominent.

Isis was originally an Egyptian nature deity but became the most popular deity in the Roman world during the time of the emperors. Called the Queen of Heaven, the Queen of War, the Lawgiver, and the Glory of Women, Isis became the benevolent mother to all. She would grant believers a happier life on earth and a life of eternal bliss after death. The story was that Isis had resurrected Osirus (her husband, and the Egyptian god of vegetation) from the dead, so she became the goddess of rebirth and resurrection. The ceremonies celebrating Isis were all about excess, wild music, and getting emotionally charged up.

The Mithras cult originated in Persia. Mithras was the god of light and truth, and acted as a kind of middleman between humanity and the supreme Sun God. He had a miraculous birth, and he accomplished many heroic feats while fighting evil, including the sacrifice of a great bull from which all good things and the promise of salvation came to

Out of the Mouths of Romans

Pliny the Elder on the importance of prayer

"It is thought that sacrifices of petitions to the gods are ineffectual without prayer. The text for invoking a happy omen is different from that for averting an ill or that for making a request. The highest officials pray in fixed forms of words, and to make sure that not a word is omitted or spoken in the wrong place, a prompter reads the text before them, another person is appointed to watch over it, yet another to command silence, and the flute player plays to mask all other sounds. There are well-known examples of both kinds of mishap, either where the effectiveness of the prayer was spoiled by a chance expletive or where there was a slip in the recitation of the prayer."

mankind. Mithras then ascended to heaven to join his father and care for the souls of those who followed him. Worshipping Mithras was very popular among soldiers who admired his heroic deeds. Mithraic rites, including baptism, confirmation, and communion were held by small groups in underground caves or in temple basilicas. Those who followed strict moral guidelines were promised eternal life. One problem—no women were allowed.

Finally, there was the cult of Cybele, which originated in Asia Minor. To members of this cult, Cybele was the great mother goddess who embodied all of the concerns of women. After she was introduced to Rome, her popularity grew fast and the cult became one of the most important in the empire. Astride the cult's growing popularity, it became commonly acknowledged that Cybele tended not only to the needs of women, but also to the outcome of crops and wars.

Mithras

The one aspect about this cult that slowed its growth and eventually led to its outlaw in the fourth century (the 300s) was that its wild rituals and ceremonies went overboard. Some of them required its followers to cut themselves, while others involved wild music, chanting, and dancing like people had never seen before.

As the empire expanded and more and more people came under Roman rule, new religious beliefs and cults were often incorporated into the existing beliefs. As long as people weren't participating in religious activities that encouraged them to think less of the state, the Roman government let well enough alone.

Christianity

Given that we've just learned about how tolerant the Roman empire was of different religious beliefs, it seems odd that Romans persecuted the early Christians. A fundamental difference between Christianity and the other cults is the likely reason why Christianity was not tolerated at first. Christians believed in one god and therefore refused to acknowledge the divinity of the Roman emperor or gods. They became branded as atheists in the Roman world, people who didn't believe in God.

Yet many Romans became Christians. When Paul, an early Christian leader, traveled through the Roman world between 30 and 60 CE he spread Christianity to all levels of Roman society. Christianity promised eternal happiness, and in many ways was similar to Mithraism. An important difference was

Out of the Mouths of Romans

Livy, Roman historian

"You will find that those who followed the gods had every success, while those who disregarded them were visited with misfortune."

Cybele

Interesting Tidbit:

Burial

Most Romans cremated their dead, but early Christians practiced inhumation (burial) because they believed bodies needed to be kept intact while waiting for Jesus's Second Coming. They buried their dead in underground cemeteries called catacombs that still exist beneath the streets of Rome.

that Christianity was open to women. Early Christianity depended upon the patronage of wealthy women.

Religious tension mounted in Rome by the second century CE (the 100s) because the growing number of Christians were openly refusing to recognize and participate in state rituals and sacrifices. This refusal was seen as anti-social and unpatriotic. It was a direct rejection of what it meant to be Roman and threatened local order. Things reached a boiling point by 303 CE when the emperor Diocletian issued edicts against Christians and their churches. Christians were told that all who would not perform state sacrifices would be put to death or sent to the mines. By 311, however, it became clear that the persecutions weren't working—Christians were peacefully going to their deaths or to the mines. The emperor Galerius issued the Edict of Toleration in 311 CE that put an official end to the Roman state's persecution of Christians.

The very next year Constantine had his vision that led him to convert to Christianity. He established the Roman Catholic Church and made Christianity the official state religion of the Roman Empire. These actions by Galerius and Constantine helped Christianity to spread far and wide.

Edict of Toleration

The Edict of Toleration, by Galerius, allowed Christians to practice their faith. This came as a surprise to many because Galerius was notorious for his persecution of Christians under Diocletian. Why did he lighten up? No one really knows, but some suspected he did so just in case Christianity was the road to heaven.

The End of the Roman Empire & Rome's Legacy

AFTER CONSTANTINE THE GREAT DIED IN 337 CE, THE once-mighty Roman empire finally fell apart over the following decades, splitting into eastern and western empires. There wasn't a leader who could hold the empire together.

Around 370 CE, the Huns—fierce, nomadic people from central Asia— swept into Eastern Europe, driving the Visigoths and other Germanic tribes south into the Roman border provinces. The migration sparked by the Huns was one of the greatest in human history. Visigoths, Vandals, Franks, Angles, Saxons, and other tribes went on the move to escape the Huns and search for new lands to settle.

Interesting Tidbit:
Barbarians

Barbarian is a Greek word that refers to everyone who did not speak Greek. Romans used the word when talking about tribal people they considered less civilized. Some say the word itself comes from "bar-bar-bar-bar" the sound the Greeks heard when listening to a non-Greek speaker.

The Barbarians

Valens, the eastern emperor, made a truce with the Visigoths, allowing them to settle in Roman territory. He promised them protection from the Huns in exchange for Visigoth men joining his army. The deal went sour the very next year when famine struck. With barely enough grain to feed the Roman army, the Visigoths starved until they rioted. Other tribes joined the Visigoths, and at the Battle of Adrianople in 378 CE, they killed Valens and three-fourths of his army.

Valens was succeeded by Theodosius, who was emperor from 379 to 395 CE. Theodosius made deals with the Visigoths and other barbarians who'd defeated his father. He allowed the Goths to settle as a kingdom under the jurisdiction of their own kings. This set a precedent for other tribes, such as the Vandals, to establish themselves within the borders of the empire. Why was this a problem for the empire? Because before long the leaders of these tribes challenged the emperors for control.

Within Roman territory, Theodosius officially banned both public and private pagan religious observations in 391 CE. Christianity was officially the only Roman religion. This drove pagan Romans—and there were still many of them—to make alliances with barbarians.

As more and more borderland passed out of Roman hands, the reach of the empire shrank. The Roman army had fewer soldiers who were Roman citizens, so it came to rely on large numbers of warriors from the barbarian tribes. Some emperors thought this would work because they believed the barbarians wanted to become Roman citizens. While this may have been true, eventually discipline within the army broke down. Because the government didn't have enough money, soldiers didn't get paid on a regular basis. It was a recipe for disaster.

Theodosius

The Empire Disintegrates

In the early 400s, Roman legions were recalled from Britain, allowing the Picts of Scotland to move south and the Saxons of Germany to cross the North Sea into Roman towns in Britain. Britain quickly fell under the control of native and Germanic peoples. Other tribes, such as the Vandals, swept through Gaul (France), then Rome's Spanish provinces, and then down through North Africa.

Meanwhile, the Visigoths united under the powerful leadership of Alaric and marched right into Rome in 410 CE. This shocked the world. Although Alaric only stayed for three days and little physical damage was done to the city itself, the psychological damage was tremendous.

Over the next half century, what was left of the western Roman Empire foundered. From 430 to 453 CE, Attila the Hun rampaged through the area, invading towns and striking fear into the hearts of millions. With the Roman army weak and unorganized, the fall of the western Roman Empire was all but complete.

Out of the Mouths of Romans

Jerome,
an early Christian writer living in Palestine,

"My voice is stopped, and sobs cut off the words as I try to speak. Captive is the city which once took captive all the world . . . The city of old . . . is fallen to ruin . . . and everywhere is the specter of death."

Interesting Tidbit:
Pagan

This word comes from the Latin word *paganus*, which means "country peasant." Why apply this term to non-Christians? Christianity was mainly an urban religion, so the country people were the last to convert to Christianity.

Who was the last Roman emperor of the west? Probably young Romulus Augustulus, a 16-year-old boy who was defeated by the German chieftain Odoacer in 476 CE. Augustulus was sent to live in Naples with a nice allowance. By that time the western empire was filled with many small, independent kingdoms.

The combination of weak leadership, the split from the east, the collapse of the military, and relentless invasions from the north and west all caused the western Roman Empire to decline and eventually disintegrate.

What was left of the Roman Empire in the east, headquartered in Constantinople, continued on for another thousand years. It was a rocky millennium filled with internal conflicts over leadership and religion, and external pressure from invaders. But what else is new?

The split between the east and west grew deeper as the years went on. In the east, Islamic armies spread their religion and culture. In the west, Christianity remained secure in its place as the main religion, with Latin as the language of Christianity.

Rome's Legacy

Reminders of Rome remain throughout the regions that were once part of the mighty empire. Buildings, walls, bridges, aqueducts, and roads built by the Romans are still used today. These physical reminders of Rome's legacy offer proof of Roman brilliance in engineering. There are also many Roman influences that permeate our religion, government, and cultures that we don't even think about.

After Constantine established the Roman Catholic Church as the official religion of the empire, the church organized itself much like the empire was organized. The pope was the head of the church in Rome. Bishops spread throughout various regions, filling roles similar to those once filled by provincial governors. This allowed the early Catholic church to thrive, keeping Roman culture intact through the centuries so that we're still influenced by it today.

Latin-Based Words in Everyday Use

politics and government
candidate, committee, congress, conservative, constitution, election, governor, legislature, liberal, majority, minority, republican, Senate

arts
actor, audience, author, camera, director, editor, literature, mural, novel, opera, statue, verse, video

science
evolution, friction, gravity, liquid, particle, radiation, solid, species, vacuum

education
campus, college, course, history, language, library, pupil, student, university

measurement
acre, century, decade, decimal, meter, mile, ounce, quart, volume

military
admiral, army, commander, company, corporal, defense, general, navy

food
asparagus, cereal, fruit, herb, onion, pork, radish

law
courts, judge, jury, legal, verdict

architecture
arch, cement, concrete, exterior, interior

The Roman Catholic mass was conducted in Latin, the language of Rome, until the 1960s. For a long time after the fall of the empire, Latin was viewed as the language of scholarship. Today, many fields, including medicine, law, and biology use specialized vocabularies that rely on Latin words.

Many modern legal notions are actually not so modern. Cicero wrote that a state without law was like a body without a mind. This makes sense. Roman law was based on common sense, with certain legal principles that could be applied to all, whether or not they were Roman citizens. These principles developed into the philosophical notion of "natural law," which forms the underpinnings for international law today.

The founders of the United States turned to Roman ideas, particularly to the writings of Cicero, when developing the new nation. Much of what they learned from the Romans influenced the writing of the Declaration of Independence and the Constitution and Bill of Rights. In many ways our representative democracy is structured much like the government of the Roman Republic.

Look around at some of our public buildings. You might find some obvious Roman influence. Thomas Jefferson designed many buildings at the University of Virginia to look like Roman temples. Public buildings like the United States Supreme Court, the New York Public

United States Supreme Court.

Library, and Boston's Museum of Fine Arts draw heavily from Roman architectural forms.

The Roman Empire lasted for about a thousand years, which is a very long time. Modern societies can learn lessons from what the Romans did right—and they did many, many things right—as well as from what they did wrong. Things were okay in the empire as long as the central authority in Rome remained just and fair. When an emperor tried to expand the empire too far, stretching its resources, or when he didn't treat people in the provinces fairly, things began to fall apart.

Q. *What lessons* has the United States learned from the *Roman Empire's mistakes?*

We can look at recent history to see other examples of empires expanding and contracting (for these same general reasons). Britain lost control over the American colonies partly because it was not treating the people in the provinces fairly (remember taxation without representation?).

Born of mistreatment, America became a haven for equality, and our forefathers made laws to ensure that it would stay that way. And although America has grown powerful as a representative government modeled after the Roman Republic, its attention to upholding the basic rights of every individual has made it even stronger than the mold from which it was cast.

Bibliography

Adkins, Lesley & Roy A. *Handbook to Life in Ancient Rome.* Facts on File, Inc., 1994.

Ardagh, Philip. *History Detectives: The Romans.* Peter Bedrick Books, 2000.

Bise, Sara C. *The Secrets of Vesuvius.* Madison Press Books, 1990.

Cambridge Illustrated History of the Roman World. Edited by Greg Woolf. Cambridge University Press, 2003.

Chrisp, Peter. *Make it Work! Ancient Rome.* Two-Can Publishing, LLC, 2001.

Christ, Karl. *The Romans: An Introduction to their History and Civilisation.* University of California Press, 1984.

Corbishley, Mike. *History as Evidence: The Romans.* Warwick Press, 1983.

Corbishley, Mike. *Ancient Rome.* Facts on File, Inc., 2003.

Dargie, Richard. *Picturing the Past: Ancient Rome.* Enchanted Lion Books/Arcturus Publishing, 2004.

Guillard, Charles, & Annie-Claude Martin. *The Romans: Life in the Empire.* Millbrook Press, 1992.

Hinds, Kathryn. *Cultures of the Past: The Ancient Romans.* Benchmark Books, 1997.

Humez, Alexander & Nicholas. *ABC et cetera: the life & times of the Roman Alphabet.* David R. Godine, 1985.

James, Simon. *Eyewitness Books: Ancient Rome.* Alfred A. Knopf, Inc., 1990.

James, Simon. *Ancient Rome.* Viking, 1992.

Jovinelly, Joann & Jason Netelkos. *The Crafts & Culture of the Romans.* Rosen Publishing Group, Inc., 2002.

Liberati, Anna Maria, & Fabio Bourbon. *Ancient Rome: History of a Civilization that Ruled the World.* Barnes & Noble, Inc., 2004.

MacDonald, Fiona, & Gerald Wood. *A Roman Fort.* Peter Bedrick Books, 1993.

Markel, Rita J. *Your Travel Guide to Ancient Rome.* Lerner Publications Company, 2004.

Morley, Jacqueline, & John James. *A Roman Villa.* Peter Bedrick Books, 1992.

Nardo, Don. *The Ancient Romans.* Lucent Books, Inc., 2001.

Nelson, PhD. Eric. *The Complete Idiot's Guide to The Roman Empire.* Alpha, 2002.

Resources

http://www.exovedate.com/ancient_timeline_one.html
A good timeline with quotes from Ancient Romans.

http://www.teach-nology.com/teachers/subject_matter/social_studies/rome/
A web site for teachers with a lot of links about Ancient Rome.

http://www.roman-empire.net/diverse/chronicle-emps.html
A great chronology of all the Roman rulers.

http://www.pbs.org/empires/romans/empire/index.html An excellent web site with thumbnail sketches of everything you'd want to know about Ancient Rome.

Glossary

abolish: to destroy, get rid of, or end.

aediles: an elected official responsible for public works and games.

agger: a mound or rampart made of earth.

alimenta: public funds used to subsidize education and food for the poor.

alliance: a friendship between individuals, groups, and/or the leaders of groups.

amphitheater: an oval building surrounding an arena for gladiator contests and other spectacles.

annex, annexation: to add on, an addition.

aptitude: skill or excellence.

aqueduct: an artificial channel to carry water from its source to a city.

arch: a curved span over an opening.

atrium: the front room of a Roman house.

augur: a priest who divined the will of the gods.

barracks: a soldiers' quarters.

basilica: a building for business and government in the forum.

benevolent: kind or charitable.

booty: valuables seized or stolen by soldiers in war.

brooch: a piece of jewelry fastened to a garment by a pin.

bulla: a locket or pouch worn by children.

bureaucratic: relating to the administrative systems of governments.

censor: an appointed magistrate who determined voting and property lists.

centurions: the Roman army's highest professional officer, originally the leaders of the centuries (units of a hundred men).

charismatic: the ability to charm or influence others.

circus: a long oval enclosure, often surrounded by bleachers, for chariot races.

cistern: a tank for storing water.

city-state: an independent nation the size of a city.

conscript: to force somebody into the military.

consul: one of two head magistrates of Rome elected every year.

coppersmiths: those who shape heated copper into crafts or tools.

cremation: the process of burning a dead body.

dictator: a supreme commander with complete control of all civil and military affairs.

divvy: to divide up to dole out.

earth rampart: a defensive wall made of earth, often topped by a low protective wall.

edict: a proclamation or law.

embankment: a hill or sloped land.

empire: territory ruled by an emperor.

equites: the wealthy class of cavalry, which became the business or middle class.

erode: to wear away or disintegrate.

ethnic: belonging to a group in a society with distinctive cultural traits.

excess: too much or more than is needed.

fasces: a bundle of wooden rods bound around a double axe with a red ribbon that signified authority or imperium.

fauna: animal life considered as a whole.

flogging: to whip or beat someone with a whip or a stick.

flora: plant life considered as a whole.

fortification: a structure built to strengthen a defenses (a wall, ditch, or rampart).

forum: the main meeting place within a Roman city surrounded by government buildings, courts, and temples.

fresco: a wall painting made while the plaster is still wet.

frieze: a scene, often one that tells a story, carved into the side of a building.

garb: manner of dress.

Gaul: the Celtic and Germanic tribes that migrated back and forth over Europe for centuries. Sometimes divided into their specific tribe names (Celts, Germans, etc).

gladiator: a trained fighter, usually a slave, who fought to the death in an arena.

hearth: the fireplace of a home, thought of as a symbol of the home and life within it.

Hellenistic: refers to Greek civilization and culture throughout the Mediterranean and Asia Minor after the death of Alexander the Great in 323 BCE up to the Roman conquest of Egypt in 31 BCE.

heir: one who inherits or succeeds to the possession of property after the death of its owner.

imperium: Latin word for "power of command," which included the power of life and death.

inscriptions: words of description carved into rock or metal.

insula: an apartment building in ancient Rome.

keystone: the V-shaped stone set at the top of an arch and cemented into place.

knead: to work dough until its smooth.

land redistribution: a plan in ancient Rome to take land from the rich and divvy it up for the poor. This plan would qualify more individuals to join the army, which required its soldiers to own land.

Latin League: a confederation of Latin cities, including Rome.

lucrative: profitable.

magistrate: someone who administers laws.

malnutrition: poor nutrition or not enough food.

megalomaniac: Greek word for "huge madness" that several Roman emperors fell into.

metalling: the top surface of a Roman road.

millennia: 1,000 years.

mosaic: a picture or design made of colored tiles.

mystery religions: secret religious practices that are only revealed to initiated members.

noxious fumes: unhealthy or poisonous gas.

pagan: used by Christians to describe someone in ancient Rome who didn't believe in religion, or believed in many gods.

paterfamilias: the male head of the household.

patrician: member of Rome's ancient ruling class.

Pax Romana: a period of time during the early empire of peace and stability.

peninsula: a narrow piece of land that juts out into an area of water.

perimeter: a boundary that encloses an area.

piety: loyalty to family or religious devotion.

plebeian: a member of the ancient freeborn lower class.

Praetorian Guard: the emperor's personal elite guards.

praetors: any of several magistrates ranking just below the consuls and acting as the chief law officers in ancient Rome.

predecessor: someone who held a position or job before somebody else.

prefect: a senior administrative or military official in ancient Rome.

principate: from princeps, "first citizen," and covers the period from Augustus (27 BCE) to Diocletian (293 CE).

provinces: a region controlled by an empire through a governor appointed by the central government.

Punic: comes from the Latin Punici, which the Romans called the Carthaginians.

quaestors: any public official in ancient Rome responsible for finance and administration in government and/or military.

ratify: to accept, usually treaties or laws.

reform legislation: laws that change things, usually to benefit those in need.

relief: a form of sculpture where the images project out from a flat surface.

republic: refers to the period of Roman history from the overthrow of the monarchy in 509 BCE to the Principate of Augustus in 27 BCE.

rhetoric: persuasive speech or writing.

roadbed: the area prepared for a road, before the pavement or concrete has been laid.

romance languages: French, Italian, Portuguese, and Spanish—descended from Latin.

sack: to destroy a captured town and steal its valuables.

sesterce (or sestertius): a coin of the realm. .

state-sanctioned: approved by the government.

succession: a series of people or things coming one after the other.

theocracy: a state governed by religious representatives.

tribune: an elected official who led a plebeian assembly and was supposed to protect plebeian interests.

veto: to deny a law or series of laws that have been thought up by others.